Salad Sensations

100 Fresh and Flavorful Recipes

Lisa Rainolds

All Rights Reserved
© 2024 by Lisa Rainolds

No part of this publication or the information in it may be quoted from or reproduced in any form by means such as printing, scanning, photocopying, or otherwise without prior written permission of the copyright holder.

This book is presented solely for motivational and informational purposes. The author and the publisher do not hold any responsibility for errors, omissions, or contrary interpretation of the subject matter herein. The recipes provided in this book are for informational purposes only and are not intended to provide dietary advice. A medical practitioner should be consulted before making any changes in diet.

Additionally, recipes' cooking times may require adjustment depending on age and quality of appliances. Readers are strongly urged to take all precautions to ensure ingredients are fully cooked to avoid the dangers of foodborne illnesses.

The recipes and suggestions provided in this book are solely the opinions of the author. The author and publisher do not take any responsibility for any consequences

Creafe Publishing

CREATIVITY ¦ FUN ¦ EXPERTISE

CREATIVITY ¦ FUN ¦ EXPERTISE

Our imprint Creafe Publishing, where creativity meets expertise, is your destination for a captivating array of books. Our extensive collection features a harmonious blend of non-fiction treasures and engaging fiction gems. We believe that learning should be an enjoyable adventure, and our commitment to 'Creativity ¦ Fun ¦ Expertise' is evident in every page we produce. Explore our catalog to discover knowledge and entertainment like never before. With Creafe Publishing, your reading journey is bound to be a delightful and enlightening experience.

Published in the United States

Copyright 2024 by Lisa Rainolds

ISBN 978-3-9071-9810-0

Table of Content

Introduction	10
Making Salads	12
Add Salad	12
Ways you can Vary your Salads	13
Tips for Selecting and Storing Fresh Ingredients	14
Recipes	16
1. Fig and Arugula Salad	17
2. Watermelon Feta Salad	18
3. Citrus Fennel Salad	19
4. Mixed Salad with Balsamic Honey Dressing	21
5. Citrus Salad with Kale and Fennel	23
6. Cucumber and Tomato Salad	25
7. Grilled Eggplant Salad	26
8. Mushroom Salad with Blue Cheese and Arugula	28
9. Artichoke Salad	30
10. Avocado and Cucumber Salad	31
11. Chicken and Broccoli Salad	32
12. Caprese Salad	33
13. Greek Salad with Grilled Chicken	34
14. Orange and Spinach Salad	36
15. Pine Nuts and Tomatoes Salad	37
16. Beets and Raisins Salad	39
17. Lettuce and Mango Salad	41

18.	Tomato and Zucchini Spaghetti Salad	42
19.	Dried Tomatoes, Raisins and Honey Salad	44
20.	Beans and Garlic Salad	46
21.	Oranges, Grapefruit and Pecans Salad	48
22.	Pumpkin and Raisins Salad	49
23.	Roasted Sweet Potato Salad	50
24.	Red Cabbage Cranberry Salad	52
25.	Carrot Black Bean Salad	54
26.	Quinoa Salad	56
27.	Cucumber & Scallion Salad	58
28.	Cauliflower Lunch Salad	60
29.	Quinoa and Scallops Salad	62
30.	Fruited Quinoa Salad	64
31.	Orange Celery Salad	66
32.	Roasted Eggplant with Tomatoes Salad	67
33.	Chickpea and Zucchini Salad	68
34.	Mediterranean Potato Salad	70
35.	Cucumber Chicken Salad with Spicy Peanut Dressing	72
36.	Grilled Chicken Salad with Balsamic Vinaigrette	74
37.	Artichoke and Tomato Salad	76
38.	Faux Potato Salad	77
39.	Orange-Tarragon Chicken Salad Wrap	79
40.	Radish Salad	81
41.	Healthy Pasta Salad with Pine Nuts	83
42.	Roasted Broccoli Salad	85
43.	Zucchini and Cherry Tomato Salad	86

44.	Pepper and Tomato Salad	88
45.	Baked Acorn Squash and Arugula Salad	89
46.	Baby Potato and Olive Salad	90
47.	Cauliflower & Tomato Salad	92
48.	Kidney Bean, Veggie, And Grape Salad	93
49.	Corn and Shrimp Salad	95
50.	Potato Mustard Salad	97
51.	Mushroom Salad	99
52.	Mixed Berry Salad	101
53.	Tabbouleh Salad	102
54.	Caesar Salad	103
55.	Pesto and White Bean Pasta Salad	104
56.	Orzo and Chickpea Salad	105
57.	Zucchini and Cucumber Salad	106
58.	Apple Radish and Almond Salad	108
59.	Pear and Pomegranate Salad	109
60.	Tropical Fruit Salad	110
61.	Apple-Sunflower Spinach Salad	112
62.	Spicy Cucumber & Corn Salad	113
63.	Seaweed & Carrot Salad	115
64.	Cucumber Salad with Minty Yogurt Dressing	117
65.	Creamy Cucumber & Dill Salad	119
66.	Cucumber & Crab Salad	120
67.	Spinach & Strawberry Salad	121
68.	Spinach, Grapefruit & Cranberry Salad	122
69.	Spinach & Pear Salad	123

70.	Sesame Crusted Tuna Steak on Arugula	125
71.	Salmon Avocado Salad	127
72.	Chickpea & Tomato Salad	129
73.	Green Bean with boiled egg Salad	130
74.	Lime Shrimp and Avocado Salad	132
75.	Black Bean, Quinoa and Mango Salad	134
76.	Broccoli & Bacon Salad	135
77.	Creamy Broccoli & Cranberry Salad	136
78.	Cheesy Broccoli & Strawberry Salad	137
79.	Spinach Salad with Warm Bacon Dressing	138
80.	Spinach & Prosciutto Salad	140
81.	Curried Chicken & Grapes Salad	142
82.	Curried Spinach & Berries Salad	144
83.	Curried Tofu Salad	146
84.	Curry Salads Curried Turkey & Fruit Salad	148
85.	Curried Creamy Tuna Salad	150
86.	Curried Peas & Cabbage Salad	151
87.	Creamy Chicken & Cranberry Salad	153
88.	Chicken, Spinach & Corn Salad	154
89.	Fruity Chicken Salad	156
90.	Cabbage Waldorf Salad	158
91.	Creamy Egg, Tomato & Avocado Salad	159
92.	Egg & Shrimp Salad	160
93.	Green Beans Salad	161
94.	Cheesy Avocado Salad	163
95.	Lettuce & Scallion Salad	165

96.	Sweet & Tangy Salad	167
97.	Warm Brussels Sprouts Salad	169
98.	Blood Orange & Avocado Salad	171
99.	Green Apple & Cashew Salad	172
100.	Apple, Blueberry & Coconut Salad	173

Appendix: Conversions & Equivalents   175

Appendix 2: Recipe Index   177

Introduction

In the past, people have often thought of salads as a common dish made of vegetables and salad leaves to have with every meal, or just as an optional food they can grab from a salad bar around the corner. However, as people become more health conscious about their health, well-being and healthy foods, salads are increasingly being considered as a main course.

Salads, as a main course have increasingly become popular, and this has brought about an enormous variety of salads into the mainstream. In most fine dining restaurants, salad chefs are hired to do the job and, in this way, salads are developed as another subject in the food line.

The best thing about salads is that they can easily be prepared by throwing together a few ingredients in a bowl and tossing with a dressing. For example, if you only pick up fresh vegetables with a sprinkling of citrus juice, you are going to have a healthy and delicious salad with few to no calories at all and still get filled up so well.

Having salads as a main course for lunch is a great trend that not only saves you time but also keeps you healthy among other health benefits. For example, fresh vegetables and leaves are full of iron, fiber and vitamins and thus keep your digestive system working properly.

Salads can be prepared using a wide variety of ingredients such as fruits, cooked meats, seafood, grains and eggs alongside vegetables. Salads are used as first course meals, side dishes, snacks, light lunches and other times as desserts too.

Health experts consider salads to be one of the most satisfying, simple but truly healthy meals. Adoption of salads as an everyday meal is one of the healthiest habits you can take up as it will be helpful in preventing various diseases such as cancer and heart diseases. Fresh vegetable and fruit salads also aid in weight loss.

If you are into salads, want to save time or get your health back on track then you have landed at the right place. This book consists of a huge variety of different kinds of salads. You name it and you have it here. In this book you are going to unravel 100 unique salad recipes from paleo, low carb, ketogenic, fast metabolism diet, kid-friendly, creative salads to weight loss salads, vegetable and fruit salads, bean salads, beef, pork, chicken and seafood salads, grain salads, and many more. So, if you want any kind of salad, it's in this book. Enjoy!

Making Salads

One of the amazing discoveries from Lesley and Susannah Kenton's book "Raw Energy" is that if you want to really enjoy the flavors of your vegetables then cut them very small. Seems silly that a small detail would make such an impression.

You don't always have to cut everything small. The trick is to prepare your vegetables differently. It's not very attractive (for the eyes, the palate or the stomach) for every salad you eat to look the same.

Add Salad

This simple rule is one that can transform your eating habits and your health. It came as a big relief to distill the path to vibrant health to something so incredibly easy. Of course, creating some reasonable variety is still key.

If you've been making the same old salad with the same bottled vinaigrette, then it is exciting to know that you can make changes easily. This is what this book is about. So, adding a salad can help you make a different taste. But just imagine for a moment that each of the 3 salads on your table is prepared with your garden variety grater. I can tell you that not only will it not look very appealing it will feel 'same old same old' (boring) in the mouth.

If every mouth feels the same, then your experience is going to lose its appeal very quickly … even if the salads are different. Having different ways to prepare your veggies is a gift. Thankfully there are lots of very inexpensive gadgets that will help you be creative.

Ways you can Vary your Salads

A major 'secret' to pepping up your experiences is in what you do. Prepare your ingredients in different ways to create interest and excitement so your food continues to surprise and delight you. Think about slicing, cubing, spiral grating, using your peeler to slice finely, supreme cutting citrus (a technique to remove the pith), juicing, mashing or even lightly grilling or steaming your ingredients.

A very useful tool is a mandolin slicer. They have all sorts of blades so that you can slice thick and thin and in between, you can use it to grate your ingredient to your desire.

You can invest a good Spiral grater, and a proper knife. There is also the handheld implement that can be used to 'crinkle cut' cucumber, zucchini and carrot. It's got a wavy edge. You can use a peeler to peel and a peeler to make strips of veggies too. But to make things a little bit faster and easier, you can go for an electric grater and slicer. This equipment is way easier to use and clean up than a food processor. Therefore, get creative. Have fun with your food. Connect with its energy, its vibrancy, its frequency and its nutrition. So, enjoy the sensual process of preparing your food and eating it.

Having a healthy enjoyment of (healthy) food will manifest a healthy relationship with all food. It will also create a healthy body shape. That's an important consideration for the many millions who need help with that.

I believe strongly that eating consistently well creates increasingly better choices and reduces cravings for things that do not serve you. This is quite literally a sign that you are becoming increasingly in tune with what you and your body needs. Eating what you love with some sensible rules to follow (mine include enjoying a green smoothie every day and 'adding a salad' to my meals) will make your health, life and shape change because you learn to bring conscious awareness into every part of your life.

Tips for Selecting and Storing Fresh Ingredients

The quality of your salad is heavily influenced by the freshness and quality of the ingredients you use. Selecting and storing fresh produce properly can make a significant difference in the taste and nutrient of your salads. The following are some tips to help you choose and store ingredients effectively:

Choose Seasonal Produce: Seasonal fruits and vegetables are typically fresher, more and often more affordable. You can make a visit to local markets or grocery stores that offer seasonal produce to get the best quality ingredients. Seasonal produce also tends to have a better taste and higher nutritional value.

Inspect for Freshness: When selecting greens, vegetables, and fruits, look for signs of freshness. For leafy greens, choose leaves that are crisp and vibrant to avoid those that are wilted. Also, check for firmness in vegetables to avoid any with soft spots, bruises, or blemishes.

Store Greens Properly: To keep leafy greens fresh, store them in a cool environment. Place them in a salad spinner or a container lined with paper towels to absorb excess moisture. Keep them in the drawer of your refrigerator and use them within a few days for the best quality. Avoid washing greens until you're ready to use them, as excess moisture can lead to wilting.

Keep Vegetables and Fruits Separated: Some fruits and vegetables produce ethylene gas, which can cause others to ripen and spoil quickly. Store ethylene-producing items, such as apples, avocados, and bananas, separately from other fruits and vegetables to prolong their freshness.

Use Proper Storage Techniques: For vegetables like carrots, celery, and radishes, store them in a container with water to maintain them. Wrap herbs in a damp paper towel and place them in a resalable bag to keep them fresh. Some fruits like berries, should be stored in a breathable container to prevent mold growth.

Prepping Ingredients: If you're prepping ingredients in advance, keep them separate until you're ready to assemble your salad. Store chopped vegetables, grains, and proteins in airtight containers to maintain their freshness and prevent cross-contamination. Prepped ingredients should be kept in the refrigerator and used within a few days for the best quality.

Use Fresh Herbs: Fresh herbs can add vibrant flavors and aromas to your salads. Store herbs in the refrigerator in a damp paper towel or in a glass of water with a plastic bag over the top. For herbs like basil, which are sensitive to cold, keep them in a cool, dry place away from direct sunlight. If using dried herbs, make sure they are still within their shelf life to ensure optimal flavor.

Recipes

1. Fig and Arugula Salad

Time: 15 minutes | Serves 2

Ingredients:

- 3 cups arugula
- 4 fresh, ripe figs (or 4 to 6 dried figs), stemmed and sliced
- 2 tablespoons olive oil
- 3 very thin slices prosciutto, trimmed and sliced lengthwise into 1-inch strips
- ¼ cup pecan halves, lightly toasted
- 2 tablespoons crumbled blue cheese
- 1 to 2 tablespoons balsamic glaze

Method:

1. In a large bowl, toss the arugula and figs with the olive oil.
2. Place the prosciutto on a microwave-safe plate and heat it on high in the microwave for 60 seconds, or until it just starts to crisp.
3. Add the crisped prosciutto, pecans, and blue cheese to the bowl. Toss the salad lightly.
4. Drizzle with the balsamic glaze.

Per Serving:

Calories: 519; Fat: 38g; Carbs: 30g; Protein: 20g

2. Watermelon Feta Salad

Time: 10 minutes | Serves 2

Ingredients:

- 3 cups packed arugula
- 2½ cups watermelon, cut into bite-size cubes
- 2 ounces' feta cheese, crumbled
- 2 tablespoons balsamic glaze

Method:

1. Divide the arugula between two plates.
2. Divide the watermelon cubes between the beds of arugula. 3.Sprinkle 1 ounce of the feta over each salad.
3. Drizzle about 1 tablespoon of the glaze (or more if desired) over each salad.
4. I don't think this salad needs any salt because the feta is salty enough, but feel free to add a pinch if you like.

Per Serving:

Calories: 159; Fat: 7g; Carbs: 21g; Protein: 6g

3. Citrus Fennel Salad

Time: 15 minutes | Serves 2

Ingredients:

For the dressing

- 2 tablespoons fresh orange juice
- 3 tablespoons olive oil
- 1 tablespoon blood orange vinegar, other orange vinegar, or cider vinegar
- 1 tablespoon honey Salt Freshly ground black pepper

For the salad

- 2 cups packed baby kale
- 1 medium navel or blood orange, segmented
- ½ small fennel bulb, stems and leaves removed, sliced into matchsticks
- 3 tablespoons toasted pecans, chopped
- 2 ounces' goat cheese, crumbled

Method:

1. Combine the orange juice, olive oil, vinegar, and honey in a small bowl and whisk to combine.
2. Season with salt and pepper. Set the dressing aside.
3. Divide the baby kale, orange segments, fennel, pecans, and goat cheese evenly between two plates.
4. Drizzle half of the dressing over each salad.

Per Serving:

Calories: 502; Fat: 39g; Carbs: 31g; Protein: 13g

4. Mixed Salad with Balsamic Honey Dressing

Time: 15 minutes | Serves 2

Ingredients:

Dressing:

- ¼ cup balsamic vinegar
- ¼ cup olive oil
- 1 tablespoon honey
- 1 teaspoon Dijon mustard
- ¼ teaspoon garlic powder
- ¼ teaspoon salt, or more to taste
- Pinch freshly ground black pepper

Salad:

- 4 cups chopped red leaf lettuce
- ½ cup cherry or grape tomatoes, halved
- ½ English cucumber, sliced in quarters lengthwise and then cut into bite-size pieces
- Any combination fresh, torn herbs (parsley, oregano, basil, or chives)
- 1 tablespoon roasted sunflower seeds

Method:

1. Combine the vinegar, olive oil, honey, mustard, garlic powder, salt, and pepper in a jar with a lid. Shake well.

2. In a large bowl, combine the lettuce, tomatoes, cucumber, and herbs. Toss well.
3. Pour all or as much dressing as desired over the tossed salad and toss again to coat the salad with dressing.
4. Top with the sunflower seeds before serving.

Per Serving

Calories: 337, Fat: 26.1g, Carbs: 22.2g, Protein: 4.2g

5. Citrus Salad with Kale and Fennel

Time: 10 minutes | Serves 2

Ingredients:

Dressing:

- 3 tablespoons olive oil
- 2 tablespoons fresh orange juice
- 1 tablespoon blood orange vinegar, other orange vinegar, or cider vinegar
- 1 tablespoon honey
- Salt and freshly ground black pepper, to taste

Salad:

- 2 cups packed baby kale
- 1 medium navel or blood orange, segmented
- ½ small fennel bulb, stems and leaves removed, sliced into matchsticks
- 3 tablespoons toasted pecans, chopped
- 2 ounces' goat cheese, crumbled

Method:

1. Mix the olive oil, orange juice, vinegar, and honey in a small bowl and whisk to combine.
2. Season with salt and pepper to taste. Set aside.
3. Divide the baby kale, orange segments, fennel, pecans, and goat cheese evenly between two plates.

4. Drizzle half of the dressing over each salad, and serve.

Per Serving

Calories: 337, Fat: 26.1g, Carbs: 22.2g, Protein: 4.2g

6. Cucumber and Tomato Salad

Time: 10 minutes | Serves 2

Ingredients:

- Salt and black pepper, to taste
- 1 tablespoon fresh lemon juice
- ½ onion, chopped
- ½ cucumber, peeled and diced
- 1 tomato, chopped
- 2 cups spinach

Method:

1. In a salad bowl, mix the onion, cucumbers, and tomatoes.
2. Season with pepper and salt to taste.
3. Add the lemon juice and mix well.
4. Add the spinach, toss to coat, serve and enjoy.
5. Top with feta cheese and chickpeas.

Per Serving:

Calories 70.3; Fat 0.3g; Carbs 8.9g; Protein 2.2g

7. Grilled Eggplant Salad

Time: 15 minutes | Serves 2

Ingredients:

- 1 large eggplant
- 1 diced plum tomato
- 1 ½ tsp red wine vinegar
- ½ tsp kosher salt to taste
- ½ tsp chopped fresh oregano
- 1 finely chopped garlic cloves
- 3 tbsp. extra virgin olive oil
- 3 tbsp. chopped parsley
- Black pepper to taste
- Capers

Method:

1. Heat the grill medium-high.
2. Prick eggplant with a fork all over, place on the grill and close the lid; cook for 15 minutes, occasionally turning, until eggplant is very soft and the skin is blistered.
3. Pull out the insides of the eggplants when they are fairly fresh and coarsely chop them.
4. Transfer the tomatoes, vinegar, salt, oregano and garlic to a bowl and toss.

5. Stir in the parsley and oil; season with more salt and pepper if necessary. If you like them, garnish them with capers. Use warm pita bread to serve.

Per Serving:

Calories: 252; Fat: 16.4g; Carbs: 18.8g; Protein: 6.3g

8. Mushroom Salad with Blue Cheese and Arugula

Time: 10 minutes | Serves 2

Ingredients:

- 1-pound portobello sliced mushrooms
- ¼ cup of extra virgin olive oil
- ¼ cup of red wine
- ¼ tsp salt
- ¼ tsp pepper
- 1 tsp thyme
- 2 cups of arugula
- 2 medium tomatoes cut into wedges
- 1/4 of a sliced thinly red onion
- ¼ cup of blue cheese
- ½ cup of croutons
- ⅓ cup of balsamic vinegar

Method:

1. Heat olive oil in a medium-hot skillet. Stir in the mushrooms and sauté for about 1 minute.
2. Add the red wine, salt, thyme, and pepper. Sauté, frequently stirring, until mushrooms have absorbed liquid (about 10 minutes).
3. Remove it from the heat. Add the arugula and the tomatoes to a large salad bowl. Arugula is covered with warm mushrooms.

4. Combine the red onion salad, blue cheese, croutons, and balsamic vinegar. Instantly serve.

Per Serving:

Calories 222; Fat 0.6 g; Carbs 58.2 g; Protein 1.3 g

9. Artichoke Salad

Time: 10 minutes | Serves 2

Ingredients:

- ¼ tsp. crushed red pepper
- ½ tsp. dried oregano
- ½ tsp. dried basil
- 2 Tbsp. olive oil
- ¼ tsp. garlic powder
- 1 cup sun-dried tomatoes, chopped
- 1½ cups marinated artichoke hearts, cut into bite-size pieces
- 1 cup fresh arugula
- ½ cup olives
- salt and pepper, to taste
- ½ Tbsp. white wine vinegar

Method:

1. Combine all the vegetables in a large bowl.
2. Mix the garlic powder, olive oil, rosemary, thyme, pepper, salt, and vinegar in a small bowl.
3. Drizzle dressing over the vegetables and serve.

Per Serving:

Calories: 356, Fat: 32.1 g, Carbs: 10.9 g, Protein: 1 g

10. Avocado and Cucumber Salad

Time: 10 minutes | Serves 2

Ingredients:

- 1 avocado, peeled, halved and sliced
- ½ red onion, thinly sliced
- 1 large cucumber, halved, sliced
- 3 tbsp. basil pesto
- 2 tbsp. lemon juice

Method:

1. Combine the avocados, onion and cucumber in a bowl.
2. Stir in the basil pesto and serve.

Per Serving:

Calories 169, Fat 144 g, Carbs 11 g, Protein 2 g

11. Chicken and Broccoli Salad

Time: 10 minutes | Serves 2

Ingredients:

- 2 cooked chicken breasts, diced
- 1 small head broccoli, cut into florets
- 1 cup cherry tomatoes, halved
- 2 tbsp. olive oil
- 2 tbsp. basil pesto

Method:

1. Heat two tablespoons of olive oil in a non-stick frying pan and gently sauté broccoli for 5-6 minutes until tender.
2. broccoli in a large salad bowl. Stir in the chicken and tomatoes.
3. Add the basil pesto, toss to combine and serve.

Per Serving:

Calories 341, Fat 28.7 g, Carbs 12.8g, Protein 11 g

12. Caprese Salad

Time: 4 minutes | Serves 2

Ingredients:

- 2 tomatoes, sliced
- 2 oz. mozzarella cheese, sliced
- 6-7 fresh basil leaves
- 2 tbsp. extra virgin olive oil
- 1 tbsp. red wine vinegar

Method:

1. In a plate, layer the basil leaves, sliced tomatoes and mozzarella
2. Sprinkle with vinegar and olive oil and serve.

Per Serving:

Calories 127, Fat 3.9 g, Carbs 23.9 g, Protein 14.5 g

13. Greek Salad with Grilled Chicken

Time: 4 minutes | Serves 2

Ingredients:

- 2 boneless, skinless chicken breasts
- 1 large cucumber, diced
- 2 tomatoes, diced
- ½ red onion, thinly sliced
- 1/4 cup Kalamata olives
- 1/4 cup feta cheese, crumbled
- 2 tablespoons olive oil
- 1 tablespoon red wine vinegar
- 1 teaspoon dried oregano
- Salt and pepper to taste

Method:

1. Preheat the grill to medium-high heat. Season chicken breasts with salt, pepper, and 1 teaspoon dried oregano.
2. Grill chicken for 5 minutes on each side or until fully cooked. Let it rest for 5 minutes, then slice thinly.
3. Combine cucumber, tomatoes, red onion, Kalamata olives, and feta cheese in a large bowl.
4. Whisk together olive oil, red wine vinegar, salt, and pepper in a small bowl. Pour over the salad and toss to combine.

5. Top the salad with sliced grilled chicken. Serve immediately or chill before serving.

Per Serving:

Calories: 350, Fat: 20g, Carbs: 18g Protein: 26g

14. Orange and Spinach Salad

Time: 10 minutes | Serves 2

Ingredients:

- 1 ripe orange
- 4 oz. spinach
- 4 oz. lettuce
- 1 onion
- 2 tbsp. Olive oil
- lime juice salt and pepper

Method:

1. Peel the orange and cube it.
2. Chop the spinach, lettuce and onion and combine them with the orange cubes.
3. Pour the Olive oil and lime juice over the salad and you are free to serve!

Per Serving:

Calories: 86 Fats: 4g Carbs: 6g Protein: 2g

15. Pine Nuts and Tomatoes Salad

Time: 25 minutes | Serves 2

Ingredients:

- 14 tbsp. pine nuts
- 3 tomatoes
- 1 oz. lettuce
- 1 big onion chopped fresh greenery

Dressing:

- 5 tbsp. Olive oil
- 4 tbsp. white wine vinegar
- 4 tbsp. lemon juice
- 15 fresh basil leaves salt and pepper

Method:

1. Roast the pine nuts in the oven for 10 min. until lightly browned and crispy.
2. Peel and cube the tomatoes.
3. Cut the lettuce, peel and chop the onion and combine all the vegetables in a bowl.
4. Let's get to the dressing now - whisk all the dressing ingredients in a food processor until they have a smooth and creamy consistency.

5. Place the dressing in the fridge for 1 hour. Pour the dressing over the salad and mix well, and then you are free to serve!

Per Serving:

Calories: 139 Fats: 7g Carbs: 11g Protein: 5g

16. Beets and Raisins Salad

Time: 35 minutes | Serves 2

Ingredients:

- 2 medium beets
- 1 sour apple
- ½ cup raisins
- salt and pepper
- fresh parsley, chopped 1 tbsp. walnuts Dressing: 2 tbsp. Olive oil
- 4 tbsp. vegan mayonnaise
- 4 garlic cloves
- 2 tbsp. mustard salt

Method:

1. Place the beets in a saucepan with water and boil over medium heat for 30 min. until soft.
2. Cool the beets by placing in the cold water for 5 min. and then grate them.
3. Peel the apple and then grate it. In a bowl, combine the beets, apple, raisins, salt, pepper and chopped parsley.
4. Let's get to the dressing now - beat all the dressing ingredients in a food processor until they have a smooth and creamy consistency.
5. Combine the dressing with the salad and then mix well. Add some walnuts on top of the beets and raisins salad.

6. Place the beets and raisins salad in the fridge for 1 hour and then serve.

Per Serving:

Calories: 170 Fats: 10g Carbs: 15g Protein: 5g

17. Lettuce and Mango Salad

Time: 10 minutes | Serves 2

Ingredients:

- 1 mango
- 4 oz. lettuce
- 4 oz. arugula
- 3 tbsp. lemon juice
- 3 tbsp. liquid honey
- Himalayan salt powdered
- Chili pepper

Method:

1. Peel the mango and cube it and then chop the lettuce and arugula and combine with the mango.
2. Pour the lemon juice and liquid honey over the salad.
3. Sprinkle with the salt and chili pepper and you are free to serve.
4. Place the mango salad in the fridge for 1 hour and then serve.

Per Serving:

Calories: 165 Fats: 4g Carbs: 5g Protein: 3g

18. Tomato and Zucchini Spaghetti Salad

Time: 15 minutes | Serves 3

Ingredients:

- 4 tomatoes, cubed
- 1 young zucchini
- 2 cucumbers
- 2 oz. walnuts

Dressing:

- 4 tbsp. white wine vinegar
- 3 cloves of garlic
- 5 fresh basil leaves
- 1 tsp. chili powder salt

Method:

1. Grate the zucchini and cucumbers in Korean style using a Korean carrot grater.
2. Roast the walnuts in the oven for 10 min. until lightly browned and crispy and combine them with the tomatoes, cucumbers and zucchini stripes.
3. Let's get to the sauce now – add the white wine vinegar, garlic, chili powder, salt and basil into a blender and smash all the ingredients.

4. Mix the sauce with the zucchini and cucumbers spaghetti and add some walnuts on top!

Per Serving:

Calories: 149 fats: 9g carbs: 14 g Protein: 7 g

19. Dried Tomatoes, Raisins and Honey Salad

Time: 10 minutes | Serves 2

Ingredients:

- 7 oz. dried tomatoes
- 5 oz. raisins
- 1 cucumber
- 1 bell pepper, orange
- 1 bell pepper, red
- 3 oz. lettuce
- 5 tbsp. liquid honey chopped fresh greenery

Method:

1. Cut the dried tomatoes, cucumber, orange and red bell peppers and lettuce.
2. Mix all the vegetables with raisins.
3. Add the chopped fresh greenery and pour the honey over the salad.
4. Place the dried tomatoes salad in the fridge for 1 hour and then serve.

Per Serving:

Calories: 165 Fats: 9g Arbs: 8g Protein: 6g

20.   Beans and Garlic Salad

Time: 15 minutes | Serves 4

Ingredients:

- 8 oz. whole grain bread
- 1 can of white canned beans
- 8 cloves of garlic, chopped
- 7 tbsp. vegan mayonnaise
- 4 tbsp. Olive oil
- 4 tbsp. sesame oil
- Salt and pepper
- Bunch of parsley, chopped

Method:

1. Cube the whole grain bread and then heat the oil and fry the bread in the Olive oil for 10 min.
2. Combine the bread with beans and chopped garlic and stew for 5 min.
3. Spoon the vegan mayonnaise and pour the sesame oil and mix well.
4. Add the salt and pepper, sprinkle with the chopped parsley and you are free to serve.

Per Serving:

Calories: 234, Fat: 21g Carbs: 33g Protein: 13g

21.   Oranges, Grapefruit and Pecans Salad

Time: 10 minutes | Serves 2

Ingredients:

- 2 oranges
- 1 grapefruit
- 3 oz. pecans
- 2 oz. sweet grapes
- 3 tbsp. liquid honey
- 2 tbsp. lemon juice

Method:

1. Roast the pecans in the oven for 10 min. until lightly browned and crispy.
2. Peel the oranges and grapefruit and cut them into segments.
3. Combine the pecans with all fruits.
4. Pour the liquid honey and lemon juice over the salad and serve.

Per Serving:

Calories: 198 Fats: 12g Carbs: 17g Protein: 4g

22. Pumpkin and Raisins Salad

Time: 10 minutes | Serves 4

Ingredients:

- 5 oz pumpkin
- 5 oz raisins
- 4 tbsp. pumpkin seeds
- 4 tbsp. liquid honey
- 3 tbsp. maple syrup
- 2 tbsp. lemon juice

Method:

1. Peel the pumpkin and then grate it in Korean style using a Korean carrot grater.
2. Combine the pumpkin with the raisins and pour the liquid honey, maple syrup and lemon juice, then sprinkle pumpkin seeds on top and serve.

Per Serving:

Calories: 194 fats: 9g carbs: 12g Protein: 5g

23. Roasted Sweet Potato Salad

Time: 26 minutes | Serves 4

Ingredients:

- ¼ cup olive oil
- 2 tablespoons lemon juice
- 3 tablespoons maple syrup
- 1 garlic clove, chopped
- 1 ¼ teaspoon dried organic rosemary
- Salt and black pepper to taste

Lemon Vinaigrette

- 1 bunch kale, well cleaned and ribs removed
- 2 ½ lbs. sweet potatoes, peeled and diced
- Salt and black pepper to taste
- 1 tablespoon olive oil
- 1 shallot, sliced
- 3 tablespoons slivered almonds

Method:

1. Preheat your oven to 450 degrees F. Toss sweet potatoes with a pinch of salt, black pepper, and olive oil on a baking sheet.

2. Bake the sweet potatoes for 20 minutes, then add kale around the sweet potatoes. Continue baking the veggies for 5 minutes.
3. Meanwhile, mix the lemon vinaigrette in a salad bowl. Toast almonds in a dry skillet for 1 minute.
4. Add these almonds, sweet potatoes, shallot, and kale to the vinaigrette in the salad bowl.
5. Mix the veggies well with the vinaigrette. Serve.

Per Serving:

Calories 157 Fat 6.1g Carbs 25.8g Protein 3g

24. Red Cabbage Cranberry Salad

Time: 12 minutes | Serves 6

Ingredients:

- 1/2 red cabbage, shredded
- 2 apples, diced
- 1 small red onion, chopped
- 2 ounces dried cranberries
- 1/2 cup walnuts, broken into small pieces

Dressing

- 2 tablespoons olive oil
- 1 tablespoon walnut oil
- 1 tablespoon rice wine vinegar
- 1/2 teaspoon Dijon mustard

Method:

1. Toast walnuts in a dry pan for 2 minutes over high heat, then transfer to a bowl.
2. Toss shredded cabbage with apple, red onion, and dried cranberries in a salad bowl.

3. Mix walnut oil, olive oil, rice wine vinegar, and Dijon mustard in a bowl.
4. Add this dressing and the toasted nuts to the salad then mix well.
5. Serve.

Per Serving:

Calories 178 Fat 11.1g Carbs 19.1g Protein 3.8g

25. Carrot Black Bean Salad

Time: 40 minutes | Serves 4

Ingredients:

Salad

- 10 carrots, peeled
- 1 teaspoon cumin seeds, crushed
- 1 ½ teaspoon coriander seeds, crushed
- 1 tablespoon olive oil
- 1 ½ cups cooked black beans
- ½ ounce parsley, chopped
- ½ ounce mint, chopped
- ½ ounce coriander, chopped
- ½ small red onion, diced
- 1 medium avocado, sliced
- Salt and black pepper to taste

Orange cinnamon dressing

- Zest of 1 large orange
- 3 tablespoons olive oil
- 2 tablespoons lemon juice
- 1 small garlic clove, minced
- ¼ teaspoon cinnamon

- Salt and black pepper to taste

Method:

1. Preheat your oven to 400 degrees F.
2. Spread parchment paper on a baking sheet.
3. Toss carrots with 1 tablespoon olive oil, cumin, coriander seeds, a pinch of salt, and a pinch of black pepper in a bowl and spread them on the baking sheet.
4. Bake the carrots for 30 minutes in the preheated oven.
5. Mix the roasted carrots with the rest of the salad and dressing ingredients in a salad bowl.
6. Serve.

Per Serving:

Calories 491 Fat 14.6g Carbs 76.1g Protein 19.2g

26. Quinoa Salad

Time: 35 minutes | Serves 4

Ingredients:

Quinoa

- 4 cups vegetable broth
- 1 ½ cups raw whole-grain quinoa
- Salt, to taste

Vegetables

- 1 medium cucumber, chopped
- 1 red bell pepper, chopped
- 1/2 small red onion, chopped
- 1/2 cup broccoli florets, steamed and chopped
- 2 medium tomatoes, chopped

Vinaigrette

- 1/3 cup lemon juice
- 1/4 cup olive oil
- 2 garlic cloves, minced
- Salt, to taste
- Black pepper, to taste

Method:

1. Boil vegetable broth with 1 teaspoon salt in a medium saucepan.
2. Add quinoa and cook for 20 minutes, then strain and rinse.
3. Mix quinoa with lemon juice, oil, garlic, salt, and black pepper in a salad bowl.
4. Stir in the rest of the vegetables and mix well.
5. Serve.

Per Serving:

Calories 389 Fat 17g Carbs 50.8g Protein 11g

27.   Cucumber & Scallion Salad

Time: 10 minutes | Serves 4

Ingredients:

- 1 ½ pounds cucumbers, cut into chunks
- 1/2 teaspoon salt
- 4 scallions, sliced
- 1 teaspoon ginger, grated
- 1 garlic clove, minced
- ¼ cup rice vinegar
- 1 tablespoon tamari
- 1 tablespoon sesame oil
- 1 tablespoon maple syrup
- 1 teaspoon red chili paste
- 2 tablespoons toasted sesame seeds

Method:

1. Place cucumbers in a colander and sprinkle a pinch of salt over them.
2. Leave the cucumbers for 10 minutes to release some of their water.
3. Meanwhile, mix scallions, remaining salt, and the rest of the ingredients in a salad bowl.
4. Stir in cucumber and mix well to coat.

5. Serve.

Per Serving:

Calories 111 Fat 5g Carb 13.4g Fiber 2.2g Protein 1.9g

28. Cauliflower Lunch Salad

Time: 20 minutes | Serves 4

Ingredients:

- ¼ cup red onion, chopped
- 1 red bell pepper, chopped
- 1 tablespoon cilantro, chopped
- 1 teaspoon mint, chopped
- 1/3 cup low-sodium veggie stock
- 2 cup kalamata olives halved
- 2 tablespoons olive oil
- 6 cups cauliflower florets, grated
- Black pepper to the taste
- Juice of ½ lemon

Method:

1. Heat-up a pan with the oil over medium-high heat, add cauliflower, pepper and stock, stir, cook within 10 minutes
2. 2Transfer to a container, and keep in the fridge for 2 hours.
3. 3Mix cauliflower with olives, onion, bell pepper, black pepper, mint, cilantro, and lemon juice, toss to coat, and serve.

Per Serving:

Calories: 102, Fat: 10g, carbs: 3g, Protein: 0g

29. Quinoa and Scallops Salad

Time: 45 minutes | Serves 6

Ingredients:

- ¼ cup cilantro, chopped
- 1 and ½ cup quinoa, rinsed
- 1 cup scallions, sliced
- 1 cup snow peas, sliced diagonally 1 teaspoon sesame oil
- 1/3 cup red bell pepper, chopped
- 1/3 cup rice vinegar
- 12 ounces' dry sea scallops
- 2 teaspoons canola oil
- 2 teaspoons garlic, minced
- 4 tablespoons canola oil
- 4 teaspoons low sodium soy sauce

Method:

1. In a bowl, mix scallops with 2 teaspoons soy sauce, stir gently, and leave aside for now. Heat a pan with 1 tablespoon canola oil over medium- high heat, add the quinoa, stir and cook for 8 minutes. Put garlic, stir and cook within 1 more minute.

2. Put the water, boil over medium heat, stir, cover, and cook for 15 minutes. Remove from heat and leave aside covered for 5 minutes. Add snow peas, cover again and leave for 5 more minutes.
3. Meanwhile, in a bowl, mix 3 tablespoons canola oil with 2 teaspoons soy sauce, vinegar, and sesame oil and stir well. Add quinoa and snow peas to this mixture and stir again. Add scallions, bell pepper, and stir again.
4. Pat dries the scallops and discard marinade. Heat another fry pan with 2 teaspoons canola oil over high heat, add scallops, and cook for 1 minute on each side. Add them to the quinoa salad, stir gently, and serve with chopped cilantro.

Per Serving:

Calories: 181, Fat: 6g, Carbs: 12g, Protein: 13g

30. Fruited Quinoa Salad

Time: 30 minutes | Serves 2

Ingredients:

- ¼ cup apple cider vinegar
- ¼ cup olive oil
- ½ cup blueberries
- 1 cup strawberry, quartered
- 1 mango, sliced and peeled
- 1 tablespoon pine nuts Chopped
- 1 teaspoon sugar
- 2 cups cooked quinoa
- 3 tablespoons lemon juice
- mint leave for garnish Lemon vinaigrette:
- Zest 1 lemon

Method:

1. For the Lemon Vinaigrette, whisk olive oil, apple cider vinegar, lemon zest and juice, and sugar to a container; set aside.
2. Combine quinoa, mango strawberries, blueberries, and pine nuts in a large container.

3. Stir the lemon vinaigrette and garnish with mint.
4. Serve and enjoy!

Per Serving:

Calories 425, Fat 10.9g, Carbs 76.1g, Proteins 11.3g,

31. Orange Celery Salad

Time: 16 minutes | Serves 6

Ingredients:

- ¼ cup red onion, sliced
- ¼ teaspoon black pepper
- ¼ teaspoon sea salt, fine
- ½ cup green olives
- 1 tablespoon lemon juice, fresh
- 1 tablespoon olive brine
- 1 tablespoon olive oil
- 2 oranges, peeled & sliced
- 3 celery stalks, sliced diagonally in ½ inch slices

Method:

1. Put your oranges, olives, onion and celery in a shallow bowl.
2. Stir oil, olive brine and lemon juice, pour this over your salad.
3. Season with salt and pepper before serving.

Per Serving:

Calories: 65, Fat: 0.2g, carbs 0g, Protein: 2g

32. Roasted Eggplant with Tomatoes Salad

Time: 50 minutes | Serves 6

Ingredients:

- 1 red onion, sliced
- 1 teaspoon basil
- 1 teaspoon oregano
- 1 teaspoon thyme
- 2 cups cherry tomatoes
- 2 tablespoons parsley
- 3 eggplants, peeled and cubed
- 3 tablespoons olive oil

Method:

1. Start by heating your oven to 350F. Season your eggplant with basil, salt, pepper, oregano, thyme and olive oil.
2. Arrange it on a baking tray and bake for a half hour.
3. Toss with your remaining ingredients before serving.

Per Serving:

Calories: 148, Fat: 7.7g, Carbs 0g, Protein: 3.5g

33. Chickpea and Zucchini Salad

Time: 10 minutes | Serves 3

Ingredients:

- ¼ cup balsamic vinegar
- 1 tablespoon of capers, drained and chopped
- ½ cup crumbled feta cheese
- 1 can chickpeas, drained
- 1 garlic clove, chopped
- ½ cup Kalamata olives, chopped
- ½ cup sweet onion, chopped
- ½ tsp oregano
- 1 pinch of red pepper flakes, crushed
- ¾ cup red bell pepper, chopped
- 1 tablespoon chopped rosemary
- 2 cups of zucchini, diced
- Salt and pepper to taste
- 1/3 cup chopped basil leaves
- 1/3 cup of olive oil

Method:

1. Combine the vegetables in a bowl and cover well.
2. Serve at room temperature.

3. But for best results, refrigerate the bowl for a few hours before serving to allow the flavours to blend.

Per Serving:

Calories: 258, Fat: 12g, Carbs: 19g, Protein: 5.6g

34. Mediterranean Potato Salad

Time: 25 minutes | Serves 2

Ingredients:

- 1 bunch of basil leaves, torn
- 1 can of cherry tomatoes
- 1 garlic clove, crushed
- 1 onion, sliced
- 1 tablespoon of olive oil
- 1 teaspoon of oregano
- 3 ½ oz. roasted red pepper. Slices
- 0.6Ibs. potatoes, cut in half
- Salt and pepper to taste

Method:

1. Sauté the onions in a saucepan. Add oregano and garlic. Then cooks everything for one minute.
2. Add the pepper and tomatoes. Season well, and simmer for about 10 minutes. Put that aside.
3. In a saucepan, boil the potatoes in salted water. Cook until tender, about 15 minutes. Drain well.

4. Mix the potatoes with the sauce and add the basil and olives. Finally, throw everything away before serving.

Per Serving:

Calories: 111, Fat: 9g, Carbs: 16g, Protein: 3g

35. Cucumber Chicken Salad with Spicy Peanut Dressing

Time: 15 minutes | Serves 2

Ingredients:

- 1 cooked chicken fillet, grated into thin strips
- 1 cucumber with peeled and cut into thin strips
- 1 tablespoon chili paste
- 1 tablespoon low-sodium soy sauce
- 1 teaspoon grilled sesame oil
- ½ cup peanut butter
- 2 tablespoons chopped peanuts
- 4 tablespoons of water, or more if necessary

Method:

1. Combine peanut butter, soy sauce, sesame oil, chili paste, and water in a bowl.
2. Place the cucumber slices on a dish. Garnish with grated chicken and sprinkle with sauce.
3. Sprinkle the chopped peanuts and serve.

Per Serving:

Calories: 720, Fat: 54g, Carbs: 8.9g, Protein: 45.9g

36. Grilled Chicken Salad with Balsamic Vinaigrette

Time: 20 minutes | Serves 2

Ingredients:

- 2 boneless, skinless chicken breasts
- 6 cups mixed greens
- 1 cup cherry tomatoes, halved
- 1 cucumber, sliced
- ¼ red onion, thinly sliced
- ¼ cup crumbled feta cheese
- ¼ cup balsamic vinegar
- 2 tablespoons extra virgin olive oil
- Salt and pepper to taste

Method:

1. Preheat grill to medium-high heat.
2. Season chicken breasts with salt and pepper. Grill chicken for 6-7 minutes per side or until cooked through.
3. In a small bowl, whisk together balsamic vinegar and olive oil to make the vinaigrette.
4. In a large salad bowl, combine mixed greens, cherry tomatoes, cucumber, red onion, and feta cheese.
5. Slice grilled chicken and arrange on top of salad.

6. Drizzle with balsamic vinaigrette and toss to coat.

Per Serving:

Calories: 320 Fat: 15g Carbs: 10g, Protein: 30g

37.   Artichoke and Tomato Salad

Time: 10 minutes | Serves 4

Ingredients:

- 1 can (14 oz.) artichoke hearts, quartered
- 2 cups cherry tomatoes, halved
- 1/4 cup sliced red onion
- 1/4 cup chopped fresh basil
- 2 tbsp. extra-virgin olive oil
- 1 tbsp. lemon juice
- 1 clove garlic, minced
- Salt and black pepper to taste

Method:

1. In a large bowl, combine artichoke hearts, cherry tomatoes, red onion, and fresh basil.
2. In a small bowl, whisk together olive oil, lemon juice, garlic, salt, and black pepper to make the dressing.
3. Pour the dressing over the salad ingredients and toss to coat evenly.
4. Serve chilled or at room temperature.

Per Serving:

Calories: 110 Fat: 7g, Carbs: 10g, Protein: 3g

38. Faux Potato Salad

Time: 20 minutes | Serves 2

Ingredients:

- ½ pound cauliflower
- ½ tablespoon olive oil
- ½ tablespoon Dijon mustard
- ⅛ teaspoon paprika
- ⅛ teaspoon sea salt
- 1 hard-boiled egg, peeled, chopped
- 3 tablespoons mayonnaise
- 1 tablespoon white vinegar
- ½ teaspoon garlic powder
- ⅛ teaspoon celery salt
- ⅛ teaspoon pepper
- ⅛ cup chopped scallions

Method:

1. Pour about 2 inches of water into a pot or saucepan. Place a steamer basket in it. Place cauliflower in the basket and cover it with a lid.
2. Steam for 10 minutes or until tender, and you are able to pierce easily with a fork. Allow it to cool completely.

3. Combine cauliflower, egg, onion, and scallion in a bowl. To make the dressing: Whisk together oil, mustard, paprika, salt, vinegar, garlic powder, celery salt, and pepper in a bowl.
4. Pour the dressing over the salad and toss well. Cover the bowl and refrigerate until you need to serve.

Per Serving:

Calories: 227 Fat: 20 g Carbs: 7 g Protein: 5 g

39.   Orange-Tarragon Chicken Salad Wrap

Time: 15 minutes | Serves 4

Ingredients:

- ½ cup plain whole-milk Greek yogurt
- 2 tablespoons Dijon mustard
- 2 tablespoons extra-virgin olive oil
- 2 tablespoons chopped fresh tarragon or 1 teaspoon dried tarragon
- ½ teaspoon salt
- ¼ teaspoon freshly ground black pepper
- 2 cups cooked shredded chicken ½ cup slivered almonds
- 4-8 large lettuce leaves, tough stem removed
- 2 small ripe avocados, thinly sliced
- Zest of 1 clementine, or ½ small orange (1 tablespoon)

Method:

1   In a medium bowl, combine the yogurt, mustard, olive oil, tarragon, orange zest, salt, and pepper and whisk until creamy.

2   Add the shredded chicken and almonds and stir to coat

3   To assemble the wraps, place about ½ cup chicken salad mixture in the center of each lettuce leaf and top with sliced avocados.

Per Serving:

Calories: 440, Fat: 32g, Carbs: 12g, Fiber: 8g

40. Radish Salad

Time: 45 minutes | Serves: 4

Ingredients:

- 1½ pounds radishes, trimmed and halved
- ½ pound fresh mozzarella, sliced
- 6 cups fresh salad greens
- 3 tbsps. olive oil
- 1 tsp. honey
- 1 tbsp. balsamic vinegar
- Salt and black pepper, to taste

Method:

1. Preheat the Air fryer to 350°F (177°C) and grease an Air fryer basket.
2. Mix the radishes, salt, black pepper, and olive oil in a bowl and toss to coat well.
3. Arrange the radishes in the Air fryer basket and roast for about 30 minutes, flipping twice in between.
4. Dish out the radishes in a serving bowl and keep aside to cool. Add mozzarella cheese and greens and mix well.
5. Mix honey, oil, vinegar, salt, and black pepper in a bowl and pour over the salad. Toss to coat well and serve immediately.

Per Serving:

Calories: 468, Fat: 38 g, Carbs: 33 g Protein: 3 g,

41. Healthy Pasta Salad with Pine Nuts

Time: 35 minutes | Serves: 4

Ingredients:

- 4 cups whole wheat penne pasta
- ¼ cup toasted pine nuts
- 4 tbsps. extra virgin olive oil
- Pinch of sea salt
- 1 bunch coarsely chopped fresh basil
- 2 cups halved cherry tomatoes
- ⅛ tsp. cracked black pepper
- 1 cup chopped fresh mozzarella cheese

Method:

1. Prepare a large pot, pour water into it, boil it, and pour in a little olive oil to prevent the pasta from sticking together.
2. Add the pasta to the boiling water, stir once, and cook for 8 to 10 minutes until hardened. Remove the pasta and set aside for later use.
3. In a large saucepan, add the pine nuts and heat them at medium high temperature, stirring constantly to prevent the pine nuts from burning.
4. Bake for about 2 minutes until the nuts smell buttery and light brown. Turn off the heat and remove from the pot into a bowl.
5. Put the cooked pasta and the remaining ingredients in a large bowl and stir together.

6. Warm pasta will melt the cheese slightly. After stirring well, divide into 4 portions. Serve warm.

Per Serving:

Calories: 388, Fat: 15 g, Carbs: 45 g Protein: 18 g,

42.   Roasted Broccoli Salad

Time: 60 minutes | Serves: 4

Ingredients:

- 1 lb. Broccoli, cut into Florets & Stem Sliced
- 3 tbsp. Olive Oil, Divided
- 1 Pint Cherry Tomatoes
- 1 ½ Teaspoons Honey, Raw & Divided
- 3 Cups Cubed Bread, Whole Grain
- 1 tbsp. Balsamic Vinegar
- ½ tsp. Black Pepper
- ¼ tsp. Sea Salt, Fine
- Grated Parmesan for Serving

Method:

1. Start by heating your oven to 450, and then get out a rimmed baking sheet. Place it in the oven to heat up.
2. Drizzle your broccoli with a tbsp. of oil, and toss to coat.
3. Remove the baking sheet form the oven, and spoon the broccoli on it. Leave oil it eh bottom of the bowl and add in your tomatoes, toss to coat, and then toss your tomatoes with a tbsp. of honey. Pour them on the same baking sheet as your broccoli.
4. Roast for fifteen minutes, and stir halfway through your cooking time.
5. Add in your bread, and then roast for three more minutes.

6. Whisk two tbsp. of oil, vinegar, and remaining honey. Season with salt and pepper. Pour this over your broccoli mix to serve.

Per Serving:

Calories: 226 Fat: 12 g Carbs: 26 g Protein: 7 g

43. Zucchini and Cherry Tomato Salad

Time: 15 minutes | Serves: 2

Ingredients:

- 1 medium zucchini, shredded or sliced paper thin
- 6 cherry tomatoes, halved
- 3-4 basil leaves, thinly sliced
- 2 tbsps. freshly grated, low-fat Parmesan cheese
- 3 tbsps. olive oil
- Juice of 1 lemon
- Sea salt and freshly ground pepper

Method:

1. Place the zucchini slices on 2 plates in even layers. Top with the tomatoes.
2. Drizzle with lemon juice and olive oil. Season to taste.
3. Top with the basil and sprinkle with cheese. Serve.

Per Serving:

Calories: 211, Fat: 21 g, Carbs: 5 g, Protein: 2 g

44. Pepper and Tomato Salad

Time: 20 minutes | Serves: 6

Ingredients:

- 2 cloves garlic, minced
- 4 large tomatoes, seeded and diced
- 3 large yellow peppers
- ¼ cup olive oil
- 1 small bunch fresh basil leaves
- Sea salt and freshly ground pepper

Method:

1. Preheat broiler to high heat and broil the peppers until blackened.
2. Remove from heat and place peppers in a paper bag. Seal and cool down peppers.
3. Peel the skins off the peppers, then seed and chop them.
4. Add half of the peppers to a food processor with olive oil, basil, and garlic, and pulse several times to make the dressing.
5. Mix the rest of the peppers with the tomatoes and toss with the dressing.
6. Season the salad with sea salt and freshly ground pepper. Serve with room temperature.

Per Serving:

Calories: 113, Fat: 9 g, Carbs: 7 g, Protein: 2 g

45.   Baked Acorn Squash and Arugula Salad

Time: 5 minutes | Serves: 3

Ingredients:

- Extra-virgin olive oil, for coating squash
- 4 cups arugula
- 1 medium acorn squash, cut into rounds
- ½ cup Brussels sprouts, shaved or thinly sliced
- ⅓ cup pomegranate seeds
- ¼ cup pumpkin seeds

Method:

1. Preheat the oven to 400°F.
2. Line a baking sheet with parchment paper. Arrange the acorn squash on the baking sheet and slowly toss with olive oil to coat well. Place in a single layer and bake for about 20 to 25 minutes, until squash is tender.
3. Meanwhile, combine the arugula, Brussels sprouts, pomegranate, and pumpkin seeds in a bowl, and toss with the dressing of choice.
4. Place acorn squash on top and drizzle additional dressing on top. Enjoy!

Per Serving:

Calories: 351, Fat: 22 g, Carbs: 34 g, Protein: 8 g

46. Baby Potato and Olive Salad

Time: 30 minutes | Serves: 6

Ingredients:

- 2 pounds' baby potatoes, cut into 1-inch cubes
- 1 tablespoon low-sodium olive brine
- 3 tablespoons freshly squeezed lemon juice
- ¼ teaspoon kosher salt
- 3 tablespoons extra-virgin olive oil
- ½ cup sliced olives
- 2 tablespoons torn fresh mint
- 1 cup sliced celery
- 2 tablespoons chopped fresh oregano

Method:

1. Put the tomatoes in a saucepan, then pour in enough water to submerge the tomatoes about 1 inch.
2. Bring to a boil over high heat, then reduce the heat to medium-low. Simmer for 14 minutes or until the potatoes are soft.
3. Meanwhile, combine the olive brine, lemon juice, salt, and olive oil in a small bow. Stir to mix well.
4. Transfer the cooked tomatoes in a colander, then rinse with running cold water. Pat dry with paper towels.
5. Transfer the tomatoes in a large salad bowl, then drizzle with olive brine mixture.

6. Spread with remaining ingredients and toss to combine well. Serve immediately.

Per Serving:

Calories: 220; Fat: 6.1g; Carbs: 39.2g, Protein: 4.3g

47.   Cauliflower & Tomato Salad

Time: 20 minutes | Serves: 4

Ingredients:

- 1 Head Cauliflower, Chopped
- 2 tbsp. Parsley, Fresh & chopped
- 2 Cups Cherry Tomatoes, Halved
- 2 tbsp. Lemon Juice, Fresh
- 2 tbsp. Pine Nuts
- Sea Salt & Black Pepper to Taste

Method:

1. Mix your lemon juice, cherry tomatoes, cauliflower and parsley together, and then season.
2. Top with pine nuts, and mix well before serving.

Per Serving:

Calories: 64 Fat: 3.3 g Carbs: 7.9 g Protein: 2.8 g

48. Kidney Bean, Veggie, And Grape Salad

Time: 35 minutes | Serves: 6

Ingredients:

- 2 ¼ cups red grapes, halved
- 1 ½ red kidney beans, rinsed and drained (15 oz.)
- 15 ounces' cherry tomatoes, halved
- 6 (6-inch) Persian cucumbers, quartered vertically and chopped
- ¾ cup green pumpkin seeds (pepitas)
- ¾ cup feta cheese
- 3 ¾ ounces baby spinach leaves
- ¾ cup Dijon Red Wine Vinaigrette

Method:

1. Place the grapes, kidney beans, cherry tomatoes, cucumbers, pumpkin seeds, and feta in a large mixing bowl and combine.
2. Place cups of the salad mixture in each of the 4 containers. Then place 1 cup of spinach leaves on top of each salad.
3. Pour 2 tablespoons of vinaigrette into each of 4 sauce containers. Refrigerate all the containers.
4. Store covered containers in your refrigerator for up to 5 days.
5. Enjoy!

Per Serving:

Calories: 322 Fat: 25g Carbs: 37g Proteins: 16g

49. Corn and Shrimp Salad

Time: 20 minutes | Serves: 4

Ingredients:

- 4 ears of sweet corn, husked
- 1 avocado, peeled, pitted, and chopped
- ½ cup basil, chopped
- A pinch of salt and black pepper
- 1-pound shrimp, peeled and deveined
- 1 and ½ cups cherry tomatoes, halved
- ¼ cup olive oil

Method:

1. Put the corn in a pot, add water to cover, bring to a boil over medium heat, cook for 6 minutes, drain, cool down, cut corn from the cob, and put it in a bowl.
2. Brush some of the oil on the skewers before skewering the shrimp.
3. Place the skewers on the preheated grill, cook over medium heat for 2 minutes on each side, remove from the skewers and add over the corn.
4. Add the rest of the ingredients to the bowl, toss, divide between plates and serve for breakfast.

Per Serving:

Calories 316, Fat 22.5 g, Carbs 23.6 g, Protein 15.4 g

50. Potato Mustard Salad

Time: 20 minutes | Serves: 6

Ingredients:

- 1 celery stalk, chopped
- 1 cup water
- 3 teaspoons dill, finely chopped
- 1 small yellow onion, chopped
- 1 teaspoon cider vinegar
- 3 ounces' vegan mayo
- 6 red potatoes
- 1 teaspoon mustard
- Black pepper and salt as needed

Method:

1. Take your Instant Pot and place it on a clean kitchen platform. Turn it on after plugging it into a power socket.
2. Open the lid from the top and put it aside; add the potatoes and water. Close the lid and lock. Ensure that you have sealed the valve to avoid leakage.
3. Press "Manual" mode and set timer for 3 minutes. It will take a few minutes for the pot to build inside pressure and start cooking.
4. After the timer reads zero, press "Cancel" and quick release pressure. Carefully remove the lid and chop the potatoes.

5. In a bowl of medium size, thoroughly mix the onion, potatoes, celery, salt, pepper, and dill. Add the vegan mayo, vinegar, and mustard; stir well. Serve warm!

Per Serving:

Calories; 14, Fat: 2g, Carbs22.5g, Protein: 4g

51. Mushroom Salad

Time: 30 minutes | Serves: 2

Ingredients:

- 1 tablespoon butter
- 1/2 pound cremini mushrooms, chopped
- 2 tablespoons extra-virgin olive oil
- Salt and black pepper to taste
- 2 bunches arugula
- 4 slices prosciutto
- 1 tablespoon apple cider vinegar
- 4 sundried tomatoes in oil, drained and chopped
- Fresh parsley leaves, chopped

Method:

1. Heat a pan with butter and half of the oil.
2. Add the mushrooms, salt, and pepper. Stir-fry for 3 minutes. Reduce heat. Stir again, and cook for 3 minutes more.
3. Add rest of the oil and vinegar. Stir and cook for 1 minute.
4. Place arugula on a platter, add prosciutto on top, add the mushroom mixture, sundried tomatoes, more salt and pepper, parsley, and serve.

Per Serving:

Calories: 19, Fat: 7g, Carbs: 6g, Protein: 17g

52. Mixed Berry Salad

Time: 1 hour 10 minutes | Serves: 2

Ingredients:

- ½ tablespoons brown sugar
- 1 tablespoon lime juice
- 1 tablespoon lime zest, grated
- 1 cup blueberries
- ½ cup cranberries
- 1 cup blackberries
- 1 cup strawberries
- ½ cup heavy cream

Method:

1. In your slow cooker, mix the berries with the sugar and the other ingredients, toss, put the lid on and cook on High for 1 hour.
2. Divide the mix into bowls and serve.

Per Serving:

Calories 262, Fat 7, Carbs 5, Protein 8

53. Tabbouleh Salad

Time: 17 minutes | Serves: 4

Ingredients:

- 1/4 cup olive oil
- 2 tablespoons freshly squeezed lemon juice
- 2 garlic cloves, minced
- Pinch salt
- Pinch freshly ground black pepper
- 2 tomatoes, diced
- 1/2 cup chopped fresh parsley
- 1 Cup dry bulgur wheat, cooked according to the package directions

Method:

1. Merge together the olive oil, lemon juice, garlic, salt, and pepper.
2. Gently stir in the tomatoes and parsley.
3. 2Attach the bulgur and toss to combine everything thoroughly.
4. Taste and season with salt and pepper as needed.

Per Serving:

Calories: 110, Fats: 12.1g, Carbs: 15.6g, Proteins: 7.6g

54.   Caesar Salad

Time: 10 minutes | Serves: 4

Ingredients:

- 2 cups chopped romaine lettuce
- 2 tablespoons Caesar Dressing
- 1 serving Herbed Croutons or store-bought croutons
- Vegan cheese, grated (optional)
- Make it a meal
- 1/2 cup cooked pasta
- 1/2 cup canned chickpeas
- 2 additional tablespoons Caesar Dressing

Method:

1. To make the Caesar salad
2. Merge together the lettuce, dressing, croutons, and cheese (if using).
3. To make it a meal
4. Add the pasta, chickpeas, and additional dressing. Toss to coat.

Per Serving:

Calories: 120, Fats: 13.1g, Carbs: 12.6g, Proteins: 7.6g

55. Pesto and White Bean Pasta Salad

Time: 25 minutes | Serves: 4

Ingredients:

- 1 ½ cups canned cannellini beans
- ½ cup Spinach Pesto
- 1 cup chopped tomato or red bell pepper
- ¼ red onion, finely diced
- ½ cup chopped pitted black olives

Method:

1. In a large bowl, combine the pasta, beans, and pesto. Toss to combine.
2. Add the tomato, red onion, and olives, tossing thoroughly.

Per Serving:

Calories: 110, Fats: 17.1g, Carbs: 19.6g, Proteins: 7.6g

56. Orzo and Chickpea Salad

Time: 23 minutes | Serves: 4

Ingredients:

- 1/4 cup olive oil
- 2 tablespoons freshly squeezed lemon juice
- Pinch salt
- 1.1/2 cups canned chickpeas, drained and rinsed
- 2 cups orzo or other small pasta shape, cooked according to the package directions, drained, and rinsed with cold water to cool
- 2 cups raw spinach, finely chopped
- 1 cup chopped cucumber
- 1/4 red onion, finely diced

Method:

1. In a large bowl, whisk together the olive oil, lemon juice, and salt.
2. Add the chickpeas and cooked orzo, and toss to coat.
3. Stir in the spinach, cucumber, and red onion.

Per Serving:

Calories: 110, Fats: 17.1g, Carbs: 19.6g, Proteins: 7.6g

57. Zucchini and Cucumber Salad

Time: 15 minutes | Serves: 4

Ingredients:

- 1 small avocado, peeled, pitted and chopped
- 1/4 cup soy yogurt
- 1 shallot, chopped
- 1 garlic clove, chopped
- 2 tablespoons fresh parsley
- 2 tablespoons fresh lemon juice

For Salad:

- 1/2 cup celery
- 1/2 cup red bell pepper
- 1/2 cup red onion, sliced thinly
- 1/2 cup cucumber, sliced thinly
- 6 cups fresh spinach, shredded
- 1/2 cup cherry tomatoes, halved
- 1/4 cup Klamath olives, pitted
- 2 medium zucchinis cut into thin slices

Method:

1. In a food processor, add all ingredients and pulse until smooth.
2. Using a large serving bowl, add all the ingredients and mix.
3. Pour the dressing over salad and gently toss to coat well.

4. Serve immediately.

Per Serving:

Calories: 660, Fats: 35.1g, Carbs: 25.6g, Proteins: 7.6g

58. Apple Radish and Almond Salad

Time: 10 minutes | Serves: 4

Ingredients:

- 2 tablespoons almond butter
- 1 tablespoon maple syrup
- 1 tablespoon balsamic vinegar
- 2 teaspoons sesame oil, toasted

For Salad:

- 1 medium green apple, cored and sliced thinly
- 6 radishes, trimmed and sliced thinly
- 1 celery stalk, chopped
- 1/4 cup pecans, chopped
- 4 cups fresh mixed greens

Method:

1. For dressing: in a bowl, add all ingredients and beat until well combined.
2. For salad: in a large serving bowl, add all the ingredients and mix.
3. Put the dressing over salad and toss to coat well. Serve immediately.
4. Shake the jars well just before serving.

Per Serving:

Calories: 575, Fats: 25.8g, Carbs: 75.8g, Proteins: 16g

59. Pear and Pomegranate Salad

Time: 15 minutes | Serves: 4

Ingredients:

- 4 tablespoons balsamic vinegar
- Salt and ground black pepper, as required
- 5 tablespoons extra-virgin olive oil

For Salad:

- 2 pears, cored and sliced thinly
- 6 cups fresh baby spinach, divided
- 1 cup fresh pomegranate seeds
- 1/2 cup walnuts, chopped roughly

Method:

1. For dressing: in a bowl, add vinegar, salt and black pepper and beat well.
2. Slowly, add oil, beating continuously until thick dressing forms.
3. For salad: in a large serving bowl, add all the ingredients and mix.
4. Pour the dressing over salad and gently toss to coat well.
5. Serve immediately.

Per Serving:

Calories: 460, Fats: 35.1g, Carbs: 35.6g, Proteins: 7.6g

60. Tropical Fruit Salad

Time: 15 minutes | Serves: 6

Ingredients:

- 2 cups fresh strawberries, hulled
- 1/4 cup fresh mint leaves
- 2 tablespoons maple syrup
- 2 tablespoons fresh lemon juice

For Salad:

- 2 cups papaya, chopped
- 2 cups pineapple, chopped
- 1 cup strawberries, hulled and chopped
- 2 cups mango, peeled, pitted and chopped
- 1 cup fresh blueberries

Method:

1. For dressing: in a food processor, add all ingredients and pulse until well combined.
2. For salad: in a large serving bowl, add all the ingredients and mix.
3. Pour the dressing over salad and gently toss to coat well. Serve immediately.
4. Cover each jar with the lid tightly and refrigerate for about 1 day. Shake the jars well just before serving.

Per Serving:

Calories: 560, Fats: 35.1g, Carbs: 35.6g, Proteins: 7.6g

61. Apple-Sunflower Spinach Salad

Time: 5 minutes | Serves: 1

Ingredients:

- 1 cup baby spinach
- 1/2 apple, cored and chopped
- 1/4 red onion, thinly sliced (optional)
- 2 tablespoons sunflower seeds or Cinnamon-Lime Sunflower Seeds
- 2 tablespoons dried cranberries
- 2 tablespoons Raspberry Vinaigrette

Method:

1. Arrange the spinach on a plate. Top with the apple, red onion (if using), sunflower seeds, and cranberries, and drizzle with the vinaigrette.

Per Serving:

Calories: 110, Fats: 35.1g, Carbs: 45.6g, Proteins: 7.6g

62. Spicy Cucumber & Corn Salad

Time: 15 minutes | Serves: 6

Ingredients:

For Salad:

- 1 medium cucumber, chopped
- 1 (16-ounce) can stewed tomatoes, drained and sliced
- 1 (8¾-ounce) can whole corn kernels, drained
- 1 red bell pepper, seeded and chopped
- 1 green bell pepper, seeded and chopped

For Dressing:

- 2 tablespoons red wine vinegar
- ½ teaspoon garlic, minced
- 1 tablespoon red pepper flakes, crushed
- ½ teaspoon ground cumin
- ¼ teaspoon dried cilantro, crushed
- Salt and black pepper (freshly ground), to taste

Method:

2. In a large serving bowl, add all salad ingredients and mix.
3. In another bowl, add all dressing ingredients and beat till well combined. Pour dressing over salad and toss to coat well.

4. Cover and refrigerate to chill for about 30-40 minutes before serving.

Per Serving:

Calories: 75fat: Fat: 0.2g, Carbs: 17g, Protein: 2.6g

63. Seaweed & Carrot Salad

Time: 5 minutes | Serves: 1

Ingredients:

For Salad:

- ¾-ounce dried wakame seaweeds, soaked in warm water for 5 minutes, drained and cut into strips
- ¼ cup carrot, peeled and shredded
- 2 scallions, sliced thinly
- 2 tablespoons fresh cilantro, chopped
- 1 tablespoon sesame seeds, toasted

For Dressing:

- 3 tablespoons soy sauce
- 3 tablespoons rice vinegar
- 1 tablespoon sesame oil
- ½ teaspoon garlic, minced
- 1 teaspoon fresh ginger, minced
- 1 teaspoon sugar
- Crushed red pepper flakes, to taste

Method:

1. In a large serving bowl, add all salad ingredients except sesame seeds and mix.
2. In another bowl, add all dressing ingredients and beat till well combined.

3. Pour dressing over salad and toss to coat well.
4. Serve immediately with the topping of sesame seeds.

Per Serving:

Calories: 62.9, Fat: 4.6g, Carbs: 4.1g, Protein: 2.1gf

64. Cucumber Salad with Minty Yogurt Dressing

Time: 15 minutes | Serves: 8

Ingredients:

For Dressing:

- 5 tablespoons olive oil
- 2 tablespoons fresh lemon juice
- 3 tablespoons plain Greek yogurt
- 2 tablespoons fresh mint leaves, chopped finely
- 1 teaspoon honey
- Salt and black pepper (freshly ground), to taste

For Salad:

- 2 cups cucumbers, peeled, seeded and sliced
- 8 cups fresh baby spinach
- ¼ of medium red onion, sliced

Method:

1. In a bowl, add all dressing ingredients and beat till well combined.
2. Cover and refrigerate to chill for about 24 hours.
3. In a large serving bowl, add all salad ingredients and mix.

4. Pour dressing over salad and toss to coat well.
5. Serve immediately.

Per Serving:

Calories: 101.6, Fat: 8.8g, Carbs: 5.5g, Protein: 1.6g

65. Creamy Cucumber & Dill Salad

Time: 15 minutes | Serves: 6

Ingredients:

- 2 large cucumbers, peeled and sliced thinly
- 1 scallion, chopped
- 2 tablespoons fresh dill, chopped
- 4-ounce sour cream
- Salt and black pepper (freshly ground), to taste

Method:

1. In a large bowl, add all ingredients and stir till well combined.
2. Cover and refrigerate to chill for about 1 hour before serving.

Per Serving:

Calories: 80, Fat: 6.2g, Carbs: 5.3g, Protein: 1.9g

66. Cucumber & Crab Salad

Time: 15 minutes | Serves: 4

Ingredients:

- 1 large English cucumber, peeled and sliced thinly
- Salt, to taste
- 1 8-ounce package of imitation crab sticks - halved
- 2 tablespoons rice vinegar
- 1 tbsp. soy sauce
- 1 tsp sesame seeds

Method:

1. In a large colander, add cucumber slices. Sprinkle with salt and toss well.
2. Arrange colander over a large bowl and keep aside for 15 minutes.
3. With paper, towels, press the cucumber slices well to remove the excess liquid. Transfer the cucumber into a large bowl.
4. Add remaining ingredients except sesame seeds and stir to combine well. Cover and refrigerate to chill for about 1 hour before serving.
5. Garnish with sesame seeds and serve.

Per Serving:

Calories: 68, Fat: 0.7g, Carbs: 10.6g, Protein: 5.1gf

67. Spinach & Strawberry Salad

Time: 15 minutes | Serves: 8

Ingredients:

For Salad:

- 1-pound fresh spinach, trimmed and chopped
- 2 cups fresh strawberries, hulled and sliced
- ½ cup pecans, chopped

For Dressing:

- 1/3 cup raspberry red wine vinegar
- ¾ cup vegetable oil
- ½ cup sugar
- 2 teaspoons poppy seeds
- 1 teaspoon dry mustard

Method:

1. In a large serving bowl, add all salad ingredients and mix.
2. In another bowl, add all dressing ingredients and beat till well combined.
3. Pour dressing over salad and toss to coat well.
4. Serve immediately.

Per Serving:

Calories: 308.4, Fat: 26.1g, Carbs: 19.2g, Protein: 2.7g

68. Spinach, Grapefruit & Cranberry Salad

Time: 15 minutes | Serves: 4

Ingredients:

For Salad:

- 4 cups fresh baby spinach
- 1 grapefruit, peeled, seeded and cut into segments
- ¼ cup dried cranberries
- ½ cup walnuts, chopped

For Dressing:

- ¼ cup olive oil
- 1 tablespoon honey
- 2 tablespoons balsamic vinegar

Method:

1. In a large serving bowl, add all salad ingredients and mix.
2. In another bowl, add all dressing ingredients and beat till well combined.
3. Pour dressing over salad and toss to coat well.
4. Serve immediately.

Per Serving:

Calories: 266.6, Fat: 23.2g, Carbs: 14.4g, Protein: 3.5g

69.   Spinach & Pear Salad

Time: 15 minutes | Serves: 4

Ingredients:

For Dressing:

- ½ cup extra-virgin olive oil
- 2 teaspoons whole-grain mustard
- 2 tablespoons balsamic vinegar
- 1 teaspoon sugar
- Salt and black pepper (freshly ground), to taste

For Salad:

- 1/3 cup sweetened dried cranberries
- 8 cups fresh baby spinach
- 1 cup red onion, sliced thinly
- 2 ripe Bosc pears, cored and sliced thinly
- 2/3 cup hazelnuts, toasted and chopped

Method:

1. In a medium bowl, add all dressing ingredients and beat till well combined.
2. In another medium bowl, add 2 tablespoons of dressing and cranberries and stir to combine.
3. In a large bowl, add all salad ingredients and mix. Pour dressing over salad and toss to coat well.

4. Serve immediately with the topping of cranberries.

*** Per Serving: ***

Calories: 244, Fat: 20g, Carbs: 17g, Protein: 3g

70. Sesame Crusted Tuna Steak on Arugula

Time: 20 minutes | Serves: 4

Ingredients:

- 20 ounces' sushi grade tuna
- 1 teaspoon toasted sesame oil
- 1/4 cup black and white sesame seeds
- pinch kosher salt
- fresh black pepper, to taste
- 5 cups baby arugula

For the soy-ginger vinaigrette:

- 1 tablespoon minced ginger
- 1 tablespoon minced scallion
- 1 tablespoon minced garlic
- 1/2 cup balsamic vinegar
- 1/4 cup red wine vinegar
- 1/4 cup soy sauce or gluten-free tamari
- 1 1/2 tbsp. honey
- 2 teaspoons toasted sesame oil
- 1 teaspoon Dijon mustard

Method:

1. Rub the tuna steaks with 1 teaspoon of oil, and sprinkle with salt and pepper.

2. Place the sesame seeds on a medium plate. Dip entire surface of the steak into sesame seeds, pressing to adhere.
3. Heat a skillet on high heat. When very hot, place the tuna steaks on the hot skillet and cook for 1 to 2 minutes on each side, depending on the thickness. Set aside on a plate.
4. Meanwhile, prepare salad and soy vinaigrette.
5. Slice tuna steaks into 16 slices and place on top of arugula. Drizzle vinaigrette over the top.

Per Serving:

Calories: 290, Fat: 8 g, Carbs: 16.5 g, Protein: 36 g,

71. Salmon Avocado Salad

Time: 25 minutes | Serves: 4

Ingredients:

- 1 tablespoon Dijon mustard, divided
- 3/4 teaspoon dried parsley
- 1/2 teaspoon kosher salt
- Fresh black pepper, to taste
- 1/4 cup chopped red onion
- 4 teaspoons extra virgin olive oil
- 2 tablespoons apple cider vinegar, recommend: Braggs
- 1/8 teaspoon garlic powder
- 1 cup halved cherry tomatoes
- 8 ounces' avocado, diced (from 2 small)
- 4 cups chopped romaine lettuce
- 1 1/2 cups red cabbage, shredded

Method:

1. Season salmon with 2 teaspoons of the Dijon, 1/2 teaspoon dried parsley, 1/4 teaspoon salt and black pepper.
2. Adjust the oven on the second rack. Broil salmon 6 to 7 minutes, until cooked through.
3. In a large bowl, combine the red onion with olive oil, 1 1/2 tablespoons apple cider vinegar, 1 teaspoon remaining Dijon, garlic powder, 1/4 teaspoon

parsley, 1/4 teaspoon salt and pepper to taste; let it sit about 5 minutes, so the flavor of the onion mellows.
4. Add the tomatoes, avocado and toss. When ready to serve, toss in chopped lettuce and cabbage, finish with the remaining 1/2 tablespoon of vinegar, taste for salt and pepper and adjust as needed.
5. Divide the salad in 4 bowls and top each with salmon.

Per Serving:

Calories: 329, Fat: 20.5 g, Carbs: 12 g, Protein: 25.5 g,

72. Chickpea & Tomato Salad

Time: 10 minutes | Serves: 1

Ingredients:

- 2 1/4 cups diced cucumbers, partially peeled
- 1 cup tomato, seeded and diced
- 1/4 cup red onion, diced
- 2 tablespoons fresh lemon juice
- 1/2 tablespoon fresh parsley, minced
- 1 tablespoon extra-virgin olive oil
- 1/2 teaspoon kosher salt and black pepper, to taste
- 15 ounces can chickpeas, rinsed and drained

Method:

1. Combine all the ingredients together and toss well.

Per Serving:

Calories: 182, Fat: 5 g, Carbs: 29 g, Protein: 6 g,

73. Green Bean with boiled egg Salad

Time: 20 minutes | Serves: 6

Ingredients:

- 6 cups string beans, ends trimmed
- 2 ounces can slice black olives, drained (check labels for Whole30)
- 3 tablespoons balsamic vinegar
- 3 tablespoons extra virgin olive oil
- 3 medium scallions, chopped
- 3/4 teaspoon kosher salt
- fresh black pepper, to taste
- 5 hardboiled eggs, peeled and sliced

Method:

1. Place green beans in a large pot and cover with water, about 6 cups. Bring to a boil, then cover and cook until tender crisp, about 6 minutes (don't overcook or they will get mushy).
2. Drain and rinse under cold water when done to prevent them from overcooking, drain.
3. In a large bowl, combine balsamic, oil, salt and pepper. Toss in the green beans, scallions and olives.
4. Mix well and top with sliced eggs. Refrigerate and serve chilled or room temperature.

Per Serving:

Calories: 176, Fat: 12 g, Carbs: 11 g, Protein: 7.5 g

74. Lime Shrimp and Avocado Salad

Time: 35 minutes | Serves: 4

Ingredients:

- 15- ounce can black beans, no salt added, rinsed and drained
- 1 cup cooked quinoa, (red or tri-color)
- 1 cup fresh or frozen corn
- 1 small red bell pepper, chopped
- 1 cup chopped fresh mango
- 1/4 cup finely chopped red onion
- 1/2 cup chopped fresh cilantro
- 1 small jalapeño pepper, seeded and finely diced
- Juice from 1 medium lemon or lime
- 1 1/2 tbsp. extra virgin olive oil
- 2 garlic cloves, minced
- 1/2 tsp ground cumin
- 1/2 tsp chili powder
- 1/4 tsp ground turmeric

Method:

1. Mix together the beans, quinoa, corn, bell pepper, mango, onion, cilantro, and jalapeño in a mixing bowl.

2. Whisk together the lemon juice, olive oil, garlic, cumin, chili powder, and turmeric in a small bowl.
3. Drizzle over the mixture and toss.
4. Refrigerate until ready to serve.

Per Serving:

Calories: 197, Fat: 8g Carbs: 7 g, Protein: 25 g,

75.   Black Bean, Quinoa and Mango Salad

Time: 35 minutes | Serves: 6

Ingredients:

- 1/4 cup chopped red onion
- 2 limes, juice of
- 1 tsp olive oil
- 1/4 tsp kosher salt, black pepper to taste
- 1 lb. jumbo cooked, peeled shrimp, chopped
- 1 medium tomato, diced
- 1 medium avocado, diced (about 5 oz.)
- 1 jalapeno, seeds removed, diced fine
- 1 tbsp. chopped cilantro

Method:

1. In a small bowl combine red onion, lime juice, olive oil, salt and pepper. Let them marinate at least 5 minutes to mellow the flavor of the onion.
2. In a large bowl combine chopped shrimp, avocado, tomato, jalapeño.
3. Combine all the ingredients together, add cilantro and gently toss. Adjust salt and pepper to taste.

Per Serving:

Calories: 164, Fat: 4 g, Carbs: 27 g, Protein: 6 g,

76. Broccoli & Bacon Salad

Time: 15 minutes | Serves: 10

Ingredients:

- 2 pounds fresh small broccoli florets
- ½ cup water chestnuts, sliced
- ½ cup red onion, chopped
- 10 cooked crispy bacon slices, chopped
- ½ cup cashews
- ½ cup golden raisins

For Dressing:

- 1 cup mayonnaise
- 2 tablespoons vinegar
- ½ cup white sugar

Method:

1. In a large serving bowl, add all salad ingredients and mix.
2. In another bowl, add all dressing ingredients and beat till well combined.
3. Pour dressing over salad and gently toss to coat well.
4. Cover and refrigerate to chill for about 3-4 hours before serving.

Per Serving:

Calories: 331, Fat: 23.5g, Carbs: 27.2g, Protein: 6.5gf

77. Creamy Broccoli & Cranberry Salad

Time: 15 minutes | Serves: 8

Ingredients:

For Salad:

- 2 large heads broccoli, cut into florets
- ½ cup celery, chopped
- ½ of small red onion, chopped
- 1 cup dried cranberries
- 1/3 cup cashews

For Dressing:

- 1 cup mayonnaise
- ¼ cup rice vinegar
- ¼ cup white sugar

Method:

1. In a large serving bowl, add all salad ingredients except cashews and mix.
2. In another bowl, add all dressing ingredients and beat till well combined.
3. Pour dressing over salad and gently, stir to combine.
4. Serve immediately with the garnishing of cashews.

Per Serving:

Calories: 331, Fat: 3.8g, Carbs: 27.6g, Protein: 3.6g

78. Cheesy Broccoli & Strawberry Salad

Time: 15 minutes | Serves: 12

Ingredients:

For Salad:

- 8 cups small fresh broccoli florets
- 1 (8-ounce) package Colby-Monterey Jack cheese, cubed
- 2 cups fresh strawberries, hulled and sliced

For Dressing:

- 1 cup mayonnaise
- 1 teaspoon cider vinegar
- 2 tablespoons white sugar

Method:

1. In a large serving bowl, add all salad ingredients and mix.
2. In another bowl, add all dressing ingredients and beat till well combined.
3. Pour dressing over salad and gently, stir to combine. Serve immediately.

Per Serving:

Calories: 257, Fat: 22.4g, Carbs: 9.7g, Protein: 6.8g,

79. Spinach Salad with Warm Bacon Dressing

Time: 23 minutes | Serves: 4

Ingredients:

- 2-3 turkey bacon slices, chopped finely
- ¼ cup sweet onion, chopped
- 2 garlic cloves, minced
- ¼ cup Dijon mustard
- 2 tablespoons sugar
- ¼ cup water
- ¼ cup white vinegar
- 1 (7-ounce) package fresh baby spinach
- ½ cup fat-free crotons

Method:

1. Heat a medium nonstick skillet on medium heat. Add bacon and cook for about 3-4 minutes.
2. Add onion and garlic and cook for about 1-2 minutes.
3. Meanwhile in a bowl, mix together mustard, sugar, water and vinegar.
4. Pour vinegar mixture in the skillet and simmer, stirring for about 1 minute. Remove from heat and let it cool slightly.
5. In a large serving bowl, place spinach. Pour warm dressing over spinach and gently, toss to coat. Top with croutons and serve.

Per Serving:

Calories: 83.2, Fat: 22g, Carbs: 11.8g, Protein: 3.9g

80. Spinach & Prosciutto Salad

Time: 25 minutes | Serves: 4-6

Ingredients:

- 6 prosciutto slices
- 1 garlic clove, chopped
- Zest of 2 oranges, grated freshly
- 2 tablespoons honey
- Fresh juice from
- 1 large orange
- 2 tablespoons balsamic vinegar
- Salt and black pepper (freshly ground), to taste
- ¾ cup extra-virgin olive oil
- 10-12-ounces fresh spinach

Method:

1. Preheat the oven to 350 degrees F. Arrange prosciutto slices onto a baking sheet in a single layer.
2. Bake for about 10 minutes. Remove from heat and let it cool completely. Then crumble it.
3. In a blender, add remaining all ingredients except oil and spinach and pulse till smooth.
4. While motor is running, slowly, add oil and pulse till well combined.

5. In a large serving bowl, place spinach. Pour dressing over spinach and gently, toss to coat. Top with crumbled prosciutto and serve.

Per Serving:

Calories: 434.9, Fat: 40.9g, Carbs: 17.6g, Protein: 2.5g

81. Curried Chicken & Grapes Salad

Time: 15 minutes | Serves: 12

Ingredients:

For Salad:

- 4 cups cooked chicken, shredded
- 2 cups seedless red grapes, halved
- 2 tablespoons fresh parsley, chopped
- ½ cup almonds, toasted and slivered

For Dressing:

- 2 cups mayonnaise
- ½ cup butter, melted (at room temperature)
- ¼ cup garlic, minced
- 1 teaspoon curry powder

Method:

1. In a large serving bowl, add all salad ingredients except almonds and mix.
2. In another bowl, add all dressing ingredients and beat till well combined.
3. Pour dressing over salad and gently toss to coat well.
4. Cover and refrigerate to chill for about 1 hour before serving.
5. Serve with the garnishing of almonds.

Per Serving:

Calories: 440, Fat: 41.6g, Carbs: 7.9g, Protein: 10.3g

82. Curried Spinach & Berries Salad

Time: 15 minutes | Serves: 6

Ingredients:

For Salad:

- 1 cup fresh blueberries
- 1 fresh strawberry, hulled and sliced
- 1 small red onion, sliced
- 6 cups fresh spinach, torn
- ½ cup pecans, chopped

For Dressing:

- 2 tablespoons rice vinegar
- 2 tablespoons balsamic vinegar
- 4 teaspoons honey
- 2 teaspoons Dijon mustard
- 1 teaspoon curry powder

Method:

1. In a large serving bowl, add all salad ingredients except pecans and mix.
2. In another bowl, add all dressing ingredients and beat till well combined.
3. Pour dressing over salad and gently toss to coat well.

4. Serve with the garnishing of pecans.

Per Serving:

Calories: 123, Fat: 7.5g, Carbs: 14.4g, Protein: 2.3g

83. Curried Tofu Salad

Time: 40 minutes | Serves: 6

Ingredients:

For Salad:

- 1 (12-ouce) package extra firm tofu, drained and cubed
- 1 red bell pepper, seeded and chopped
- 1 large carrot, peeled and grated
- ¼ cup dates, pitted and chopped
- 1 large scallion, chopped
- ¼ cup peanuts, chopped

For Dressing:

- 2 tablespoons mayonnaise
- 1 tablespoon soy sauce
- 1 tablespoon distilled white vinegar
- 1 tablespoon fresh lemon juice
- 1 teaspoon curry powder
- ¼ teaspoon red pepper flakes, crushed

Method:

1. Preheat the oven to 350 degrees F. Lightly, grease a baking sheet.
2. Place tofu cubes onto prepared baking sheet in a single layer.

3. Bake for about 25 minutes, flipping once in the middle way.
4. Remove the tofu from oven and transfer into a large bowl. Let it cool completely.
5. Add all salad ingredients in the bowl with tofu and mix.
6. In another bowl, add all dressing ingredients and beat till well combined.
7. Pour dressing over salad and gently toss to coat well. Serve immediately.

Per Serving:

Calories: 149, Fat: 9.5g, Carbs: 11.6g, Protein: 6.8g

84. Curry Salads Curried Turkey & Fruit Salad

Time: 15 minutes | Serves: 12

Ingredients:

For Dressing:

- 1/3 cup reduced-fat sour cream
- 1 tablespoon honey
- 1 tablespoon fresh lemon juice
- 2 tablespoons mango chutney
- ¼ teaspoon curry powder

For Salad:

- 4 cups cooked turkey, chopped
- 1 cup pineapple chunks
- 1 cup orange segments, seeded
- 1 cup celery, chopped
- 1 cup red bell pepper, seeded and chopped
- ½ cup scallion, chopped

Method:

1. In a medium bowl, add all dressing ingredients and beat till well combined.
2. Refrigerate before serving. In a large serving bowl, add all salad ingredients and mix.

3. Pour dressing over salad and gently toss to coat well.
4. Cover and refrigerate to chill for about 1 hour before serving.

Per Serving:

Calories: 126, Fat: 3.2g, Carbs: 9.6g, Protein: 14.4g

85. Curried Creamy Tuna Salad

Time: 15 minutes | Serves: 4

Ingredients:

- 1 (7ounce) can white tuna, (water packed) drained and flaked
- 3 tablespoons sweet pickle relish
- 1/3 cup mayonnaise
- 1 tablespoon parmesan cheese, grated
- ¼ teaspoon curry powder
- 1 teaspoon dried dill weed
- 1 tablespoon dried parsley, crushed
- 1/8 teaspoon dried onion flakes, minced
- Pinch of garlic powder

Method:

2. In a serving bowl, add all ingredients and gently stir to combine.
3. Serve immediately.

Per Serving:

Calories: 228, Fat: 17.3g, Carbs: 5.3g, Protein: 13.4g

86. Curried Peas & Cabbage Salad

Time: 15 minutes | Serves: 8

Ingredients:

For Salad:

- 2 cups cabbage, shredded finely
- 1 (10-ounce) package frozen peas, thawed
- 1 scallion, chopped
- ¾ cup salted peanuts, chopped

For Dressing:

- ¼ cup mayonnaise
- ¼ cup sour cream
- 1 teaspoon white wine vinegar
- 1 teaspoon prepared mustard
- ¼ teaspoon curry powder
- Salt, to taste

Method:

1. In a large serving bowl, add all salad ingredients except peanuts and mix.
2. In another bowl, add all dressing ingredients and beat till well combined.
3. Pour dressing over salad and gently toss to coat well.

4. Cover and refrigerate to chill for about 1 hour before serving.
5. Serve with the garnishing of peanuts.

Per Serving:

Calories: 177, Fat: 13.9g, Carbs: 9.5g, Protein: 5.6g

87. Creamy Chicken & Cranberry Salad

Time: 15 minutes | Serves: 4

Ingredients:

- 3 cups cooked chicken, chopped
- ½ cup sweetened dried cranberries
- 1 red bell pepper, seeded and chopped
- 2 large celery stalks, chopped
- ¼ of red onion, chopped
- 1/3 cup sour cream
- 1/3 cup mayonnaise
- Salt and black pepper (freshly ground), to taste
- 1/3 cup almonds, toasted and chopped
- 4-ounce feta cheese, crumbled

Method:

1. In a large bowl, add all ingredients except almonds and cheese and mix till well combined.
2. Cover and refrigerate to chill for 6-8 hours before serving.
3. Top with almonds and cheese just before serving.

Per Serving:

Calories: 611, Fat: 44.3g, Carbs: 20.2g, Protein: 33.1g

88. Chicken, Spinach & Corn Salad

Time: 15 minutes | Serves: 4

Ingredients:

For Salad:

- 1½ cups cooked chicken, cubed
- ½ cup corn kernels
- 1 cup cherry tomatoes, halved
- 1 large avocado, peeled, pitted and chopped
- 8 cups fresh spinach, chopped
- 1/3 cup goat cheese, rumbled
- ¼ cup pine nuts

For Dressing:

- 1 tablespoon Dijon mustard
- 2 tablespoons extra-virgin olive oil
- 3 tablespoons white wine vinegar
- Salt and black pepper (freshly ground), to taste

Method:

1. In a large bowl, mix together all salad ingredients except pine nuts.
2. In another bowl, add all dressing ingredients and beat till well combined.
3. Pour dressing over salad and stir to combine.
4. Serve immediately with the garnishing of pine nuts.

Per Serving:

Calories: 441, Fat: 31.8g, Carbs: 17.9g, Protein: 25.8g

89. Fruity Chicken Salad

Time: 15 minutes | Serves: 6

Ingredients:

For Salad:

- 1 pound cooked chicken breast, cubed
- ¾ cup seedless green grapes, halved
- 1 medium apple, cored and chopped
- 4 celery stalks, chopped
- ¼ cup scallion, chopped
- ¼ cup almonds, toasted and chopped
- ¼ cup unsweetened flaked coconut, toasted

For Dressing:

- 1/3 cup unsweetened coconut milk
- 6-ounces plain Greek yogurt
- 1 tablespoon Dijon mustard
- 1 tablespoon cider vinegar
- 1 tablespoon fresh lemon juice
- ½ teaspoon garlic powder

Method:

1. In a large bowl, mix together all salad ingredients except coconut.
2. In another bowl, add all dressing ingredients and beat till well combined.

3. Pour dressing over salad and stir to combine.
4. Serve with the topping of flaked coconut.

Per Serving:

Calories: 205, Fat: 10.1g, Carbs: 13.6g, Protein: 15.6g

90. Cabbage Waldorf Salad

Time: 15 minutes | Serves: 4-6

Ingredients:

- 4 apples, cored and chopped
- 6 celery stalks, chopped
- ¼ head of savory cabbage
- ½ cup walnuts, chopped
- 1 tablespoon white sugar
- 1/3 cup mayonnaise
- Salt, to taste

Method:

1. In a large bowl, add all ingredients and mix till well combined.
2. Serve immediately or you can serve this salad after chilling.

Per Serving:

Calories: 336, Fat: 24.5g, Carbs: 30g, Protein: 4.3g

91. Creamy Egg, Tomato & Avocado Salad

Time: 15 minutes | Serves: 6

Ingredients:

- 6 hard-boiled eggs, peeled and chopped
- 1 cup tomatoes, seeded and chopped
- 2 large avocados, peeled, pitted and chopped
- ½ cup red onion, chopped
- 2 tablespoons mayonnaise
- 2 tablespoons sour cream
- 1 tablespoon fresh lemon juice
- 10 drops hot sauce
- Salt and black pepper (freshly ground), to taste

Method:

1. In a large serving bowl, add all ingredients and gently stir to combine.
2. Serve immediately.

Per Serving:

Calories: 284, Fat: 23.9g, Carbs: 11.7g, Protein: 8.8g

92. Egg & Shrimp Salad

Time: 15 minutes | Serves: 4

Ingredients:

- 4 hard-boiled eggs, peeled and chopped
- 1 pound cooked shrimp, peeled, deveined and chopped
- 1 sprig fresh dill, chopped
- ¼ cup mayonnaise
- 1 teaspoon Dijon mustard
- 4 fresh lettuce leaves

Method:

1. In a large serving bowl, add all ingredients except lettuce and gently stir to combine.
2. Serve immediately over the bed of lettuce leaves.

Per Serving:

Calories: 292, Fat: 17.5g, Carbs: 1.6g, Protein: 30.3g

93. Green Beans Salad

Time: 15 minutes | Serves: 4

Ingredients:

For Salad:

- ½ pound boiled green beans, halved
- 4 cups mixed baby salad greens
- 2-ounces feta cheese, crumbled
- 1/3 cup dried cranberries (if desired)

For Dressing:

- 2 tablespoons extra-virgin olive oil
- 1 tablespoon fresh orange juice
- 1 tablespoon balsamic vinegar
- ½ teaspoon fennel seeds
- Salt and black pepper (freshly ground), to taste

Method:

1. In a large serving bowl, add all salad ingredients except cranberries and mix.
2. In another bowl, add all dressing ingredients and beat till well combined.
3. Pour dressing over salad and gently toss to coat well.
4. Serve immediately with the topping of cranberries.

Per Serving:

Calories: 160, Fat: 10.1g, Carbs: 15.5g, Protein: 3.9g

94. Cheesy Avocado Salad

Time: 10 minutes | Serves: 4

Ingredients:

For Salad:

- 1 large avocado, peeled, pitted and sliced
- 6 cups frisee leaves, torn
- ¼ cup blue cheese, crumbled
- ¼ cup almonds, toasted and chopped

For Dressing:

- 1½ tablespoons red wine vinegar
- 3 tablespoons olive oil
- ½ teaspoon honey
- ¼ teaspoon Dijon mustard
- Salt and black pepper (freshly ground), to taste

Method:

1. In a large serving bowl, add all salad ingredients except almonds and mix.
2. In another bowl, add all dressing ingredients and beat till well combined.
3. Pour dressing over salad and gently toss to coat well.
4. Serve immediately with the topping of almonds.

Per Serving:

Calories: 332, Fat: 31g, Carbs: 10g, Protein: 7g

95. Lettuce & Scallion Salad

Time: 10 minutes | Serves: 4

Ingredients:

For Salad:

- 1 head Boston lettuce, torn
- 2 large scallions (green part), chopped
- 1 small tarragon sprig, for garnishing

For Dressing:

- ½ cup fresh flat leaf parsley leaves, roughly chopped
- 2 teaspoons fresh tarragon leaves, roughly chopped
- 2 teaspoons white wine vinegar
- 3 tablespoons vegetable oil
- 1 tablespoon water
- Salt and black pepper (freshly ground), to taste

Method:

1. In a large serving bowl, add lettuce and scallion and mix.
2. In a blender, add all dressing ingredients and pulse till well combined and smooth.
3. Pour dressing over salad and gently toss to coat well.
4. Serve immediately with the garnishing of tarragon.

Per Serving:

Calories: 332, Fat: 31g, Carbs: 10g, Protein: 7g

96. Sweet & Tangy Salad

Time: 15 minutes | Serves: 4

Ingredients:

For Dressing:

- ½ cup lemonade
- 1 tablespoon apple cider vinegar
- 1 tablespoon peanut oil
- 1 tablespoon fresh lemon juice
- 2 tablespoons honey
- ½ teaspoon hot sauce
- ½ teaspoon celery seeds
- Salt and black pepper (freshly ground), to taste

For Salad:

- ½ green apple, cored and sliced
- 16 green seedless grapes, halved
- ½ cup frozen peas, thawed
- ½ English cucumber, chopped
- ½ green bell pepper, seeded and chopped
- 2 stalks celery, chopped
- 6 cups romaine lettuce, torn

- 2 scallions (green part)
- ½ cup blue cheese, crumbled

Method:

1. In a blender, add all dressing ingredients and pulse till well combined and smooth. Keep aside for 30 minutes to mingle the flavors.
2. In a large serving bowl, add all salad ingredients except cheese and mix.
3. Pour dressing over salad and gently toss to coat well.
4. Serve immediately with the topping of cheese.

Per Serving:

Calories: 200, Fat: 8.9g, Carbs: 26.7g, Protein: 6.5g

97. Warm Brussels Sprouts Salad

Time: 20 minutes | Serves: 8

Ingredients:

- 6 smoked bacon slices
- 1½ tablespoons maple syrup
- 1/3 cup white wine vinegar
- 2 teaspoons Dijon mustard
- Salt and black pepper (freshly ground), to taste
- ¾ pound Brussels sprouts, sliced
- 6 cups romaine lettuce, torn
- ¼ cup pecans, toasted and chopped

Method:

1. Heat a large nonstick skillet on medium-high heat. Add bacon and cook, stirring occasionally for about 5 minutes or till crisp.
2. Transfer the bacon into a bowl. Drain the excess fat, reserving 2 tablespoons in the skillet.
3. Reduce the heat to medium-low. Stir in maple syrup, vinegar, mustard, salt and black pepper.
4. Add Brussels sprouts and cook, stirring for 1 minute. Cover and cook for about 2 to 3 minutes.
5. Transfer the Brussels sprouts mixture in a large serving bowl. Add lettuce and mix. Top with bacon and pecans and serve immediately.

Per Serving:

Calories: 116, Fat: 8.1g, Carbs: 8.4g, Protein: 4.1g

98. Blood Orange & Avocado Salad

Time: 15 minutes | Serves: 4

Ingredients:

- 1 blood orange, peeled, seeded and cut into small pieces
- 1 avocado, peeled, pitted and cubed
- 1 tablespoon extra-virgin olive oil
- Pinch of Salt and black pepper (freshly ground), to taste

Method:

1. In a large bowl, add all ingredients and toss to coat well.
2. Serve immediately and enjoy.

Per Serving:

Calories: 522, Fat: 43.2g, Carbs: 36.9g, Protein: 5.6g

99. Green Apple & Cashew Salad

Time: 15 minutes | Serves: 1

Ingredients:

- ½ of large green apple, cored and sliced
- 2 cups mixed fresh greens
- 1 tablespoon unsalted cashews
- 1 tablespoon apple cider vinegar

Method:

1. In a serving bowl, mix together apple, greens and cashews.
2. Drizzle with apple cider vinegar and serve immediately.

Per Serving:

Calories: 118, Fat: 4g, Carbs: 19g, Protein: 3g

100. Apple, Blueberry & Coconut Salad

Time: 15 minutes | Serves: 4

Ingredients:

For Dressing:

- 3 tablespoons fat-free vanilla yogurt
- 3 tablespoons honey

For Salad:

- 2 small delicious red apples, cored and chopped
- 1 cup fresh blueberries
- 1 avocado, peeled, pitted and chopped
- 1 cup coconut flakes
- ½ cup almonds, slivered

Method:

1. In a large bowl, add yogurt and honey and stir to combine.
2. Add all salad ingredients and gently, stir to combine.
3. Serve immediately.

Per Serving:

Calories: 349, Fat: 19.6g, Carbs: 44.1g, Protein: 5.5g

Appendix: Conversions & Equivalents

Volume Equivalents (Liquid)		
Standard	Us Standard (Ounces)	Metric (Approximate)
2 tablespoons	1 fl. oz.	30 mL
¼ cup	2 fl. oz.	60 mL
½ cup	4 fl. oz.	120 mL
1 cup	8 fl. oz.	240 mL
1½ cups	12 fl. oz.	355 mL
2 cups or 1 pint	16 fl. oz.	475 mL
4 cups or 1 quart	32 fl. oz.	1 L
1 gallon	128 fl. oz.	4 L

Oven Temperatures	
Fahrenheit (F)	Celsius (C) (Approximate)
250°	120°
300°	150°
325°	165°
350°	180°
375°	190°
400°	200°
425°	220°
450°	230°

Volume Equivalents (Dry)	
Standard	**Metric (Approximate)**
⅛ teaspoon	0.5 mL
¼ teaspoon	1 mL
½ teaspoon	2 mL
¾ teaspoon	4 mL
1 teaspoon	5 mL
1 tablespoon	15 mL
¼ cup	59 mL
⅓ cup	79 mL
½ cup	118 mL
⅔ cup	156 mL
¾ cup	177 mL
1 cup	235 mL
2 cups or 1 pint	475 mL
3 cups	700 mL
4 cups or 1 quart	1 L

Weight Equivalents	
Standard	**Metric (Approximate)**
½ ounce	15 g
1 ounce	30 g
2 ounces	60 g
4 ounces	115 g
8 ounces	225 g
12 ounces	340 g
16 ounces or 1 pound	455 g

Appendix 2: Recipe Index

Apple Radish and Almond Salad... 108
Apple, Blueberry & Coconut Salad 173
Apple-Sunflower Spinach Salad..... 112
Artichoke and Tomato Salad.............76
Artichoke Salad 30
Avocado and Cucumber Salad..........31
Baby Potato and Olive Salad.............90
Baked Acorn Squash and Arugula Salad..................89
Beans and Garlic Salad......................46
Beets and Raisins Salad 39
Black Bean, Quinoa and Mango Salad 134
Blood Orange & Avocado Salad ... 171
Broccoli & Bacon Salad 135
Cabbage Waldorf Salad 158
Caesar Salad 103
Caprese Salad....................................33
Carrot Black Bean Salad....................54
Cauliflower Lunch Salad 60
Cheesy Avocado Salad 163
Chicken and Broccoli Salad...............32
Chicken, Spinach & Corn Salad..... 154
Chickpea and Zucchini Salad 68
Citrus Fennel Salad 19
Citrus Salad with Kale and Fennel ...23
Corn and Shrimp Salad 95
Creamy Broccoli & Cranberry Salad 136
Creamy Cucumber & Dill Salad..... 119
Creamy Egg, Tomato & Avocado Salad.............. 159
Cucumber & Crab Salad 120
Cucumber & Scallion Salad 58
Cucumber and Tomato Salad........... 25
Cucumber Chicken Salad with Spicy Peanut Dressing............................ 72
Cucumber Salad with Minty Yogurt Dressing................. 117
Curried Chicken & Grapes Salad... 142
Curried Creamy Tuna Salad............ 150
Curried Peas & Cabbage Salad....... 151
Curried Spinach & Berries Salad.... 144
Curried Tofu Salad........................... 146
Curry Salads Curried Turkey & Fruit Salad............................... 148
Dried Tomatoes, Raisins and Honey Salad................................ 44
Egg & Shrimp Salad......................... 160
Faux Potato Salad............................. 77
Fig and Arugula Salad...................... 17
Fruited Quinoa Salad...................... 64
Fruity Chicken Salad....................... 156
Greek Salad with Grilled Chicken ... 34
Green Apple & Cashew Salad........ 172
Green Bean with boiled egg Salad. 130
Green Beans Salad 161
Grilled Chicken Salad with Balsamic Vinaigrette........................ 74
Grilled Eggplant Salad...................... 26
Kidney Bean, Veggie, And Grape Salad 93
Lettuce & Scallion Salad.................. 165
Lettuce and Mango Salad................ 41
Lime Shrimp and Avocado Salad .. 132
Mediterranean Potato Salad.............. 70
Mixed Berry Salad 101

Mixed Salad with Balsamic Honey Dressing 21
Mushroom Salad 99
Mushroom Salad with Blue Cheese and Arugula 28
Orange and Spinach Salad 36
Orange Celery Salad 66
Oranges, Grapefruit and Pecans Salad 48
Orange-Tarragon Chicken Salad Wrap 79
Orzo and Chickpea Salad 105
Pear and Pomegranate Salad 109
Pepper and Tomato Salad 88
Pesto and White Bean Pasta Salad 104
Pine Nuts and Tomatoes Salad 37
Potato Mustard Salad 97
Pumpkin and Raisins Salad 49
Quinoa and Scallops Salad 62
Quinoa Salad 56
Red Cabbage Cranberry Salad 52
Roasted Broccoli Salad 85
Roasted Eggplant with Tomatoes Salad 67
Roasted Sweet Potato Salad 50
Salmon Avocado Salad 127
Seaweed & Carrot Salad 115
Sesame Crusted Tuna Steak on Arugula 125
Spicy Cucumber & Corn Salad 113
Spinach & Apple Salad 123
Spinach & Prosciutto Salad 140
Spinach & Strawberry Salad 121
Spinach Salad with Warm Bacon Dressing 138
Spinach, Grapefruit & Cranberry Salad 122
Sweet & Tangy Salad 167
Tabbouleh Salad 102
Tomato and Zucchini Spaghetti Salad 42
Tropical Fruit Salad 110
Warm Brussels Sprouts Salad 169
Watermelon Feta Salad 18
Zucchini and Cherry Tomato Salad 86
Zucchini and Cucumber Salad 106

www.ingramcontent.com/pod-product-compliance
Ingram Content Group UK Ltd.
Pitfield, Milton Keynes, MK11 3LW, UK
UKHW052120230426
12049UKWH00009BA/136

9 783907 198100